Irene Merrill Mason

As I Remember It

An Autobiography

By

Irene Merrill Mason

Growing Up in 1890's Iowa

Compiled by

David M. Mason & Marilyn M. LaCamera

Marilyn LaCamera

[signature]

ISBN 978-1494986407

CONTENTS

ACKNOWLEDGEMENTS

We would first like to acknowledge the foresight of our mother, Mary E. Mason, for saving the manuscript, allowing us to publish this book.

And the Hennepin County Library archives in Minneapolis and the Kendall Young Library in Webster City which provided much of the genealogical documentation and photographs used in the book. In particular, Librarian Rebecca Philipsen of the Kendall Young Library who has provided many of the photographs used in the book and many resources to supplement the Merrill family history.

We would also like to acknowledge our cousins, Michael, Gay and Terry Finlayson for preserving our grandmother's photos and recordings to use in compiling this book.

And finally The Church of Jesus Christ of Latter Day Saints whose genealogical records provided much of the documentation for the Merrill family history.

INTRODUCTION

This is not a "polished" book. It is written exactly as our grandmother wrote her manuscript in the 1890's, much in the same way that she spoke. Format, sentence structure, spellings, punctuations, outdated or "coined" words and chapter organization are all her choice. Our intent is to give the reader a sense of feeling for the time of her stories and her way of writing.

Considerable research has been done to determine who some of the people are that Gram only refers to by their nickname or first name. The photographs used are from the period and most are of the exact location Gram writes about. For those wanting more background we have included a family chronology in the back of the book. The numbered notes will also help you if you want more information.

The 1890's were a time of prosperity in the United States. Although initially there was no inside plumbing, electricity, telephones, or automobiles, these things were just coming to be; but there was steam. With the expansion of the railroads and the industrialization in the east, the population spread west and farmers became necessary to support the ever expanding country.

With that growth and travel, the need for places to sleep and eat became ever more important. Hence the need for hotels of which our great grandfather and both great great grandfathers on the Merrill side were involved in running. The tales that follow are of our grandmother, Irene Merrill, growing up in a hotel and with her father and his father both running hotels in

Iowa and Minneapolis during the end of the 19th century.

It was these stories we heard as children that prompted us to publish Gram's manuscript in this book. One story she told that we recall, that is not in her manuscript, was when they were living in the Willson Hotel. She would often go up into the hotel's cupola to escape from her brother and sisters and any possible work to be done.

It was this one time that she heard her name being called from down below, over and over, until it stopped. Shortly after, she heard the sound of a wagon leaving the yard below and she looked out the window to see the entire family going off.

Later she found out they had gone on a picnic, an adventure she loved, but not being able to find her they had gone without her. A lesson she learned – not to ignore someone when they call your name.

This book is about many of those stories, told in her own words and writings.

GRANDFATHERS ARE THE NICEST PEOPLE

That was my grandfather.[1] A kind and gentle man, he was my childhood favorite. Best of all, he was fun loving. There was a part of him that never grew up. To the end of his 78 years he remained a small boy at heart.

I don't remember the color of his eyes, but they were possessed of a perennial twinkle. He had a delightful chuckle that bubbled up when anything tickled him, which was often. For a grandfather, he was exactly what any small girl might have ordered. A sort of Santa Claus and grandfather combined.

I followed him about like a little puppy. He always had a striped bag of peppermints in his coat pocket which he doled out generously. But that wasn't why I followed him. He was just fun to be with.

He loved to play jokes, or catch people up on something they'd say. Like the time I, sitting in his chair when he entered the room, piped up, "Do you want your chair back, Grandpa?"

"No!" he said, his eyes twinkling, "I want my whole chair, not just the back!" Or the day he told me, face sober as a judge, "They're selling stamps today, thirteen for a cent and a quarter, Irene. You'd better run down to the Post Office and get some." My eyes popped. "Honest? Will you give me the money?" But Grandma, always impatient with his foolery, quickly assured me that thirteen stamps could be bought any day for 25 cents and one penny – back then, mind you!

One day when I was mourning over the loss of a dime, he told me not to mind, that when I went home he'd send me a whole box of dimes. As my going home was imminent, and as I immediately envisioned a box that would hold hundreds of dimes, that promise stopped my tears instantly. True to his word, my box of dimes came. A cute little wooden box, size of a dime bank, that held exactly one dollar's worth of dimes!

I spent much of my young life with my grandparents. Every time Mother was due to have a  baby I'd stay with them. As Mother had a new baby about every other summer, theirs almost became a second home. Since I got much more attention when with them than at home, that suited me fine.

I recall once—I can see that scene as if it were a picture on my wall – I was standing at the office desk in my grandparents' Minneapolis hotel when Grandfather, looking up from a telegram he was reading, informed me that I had a new baby sister.

If you think that pleased me, you're wrong. I stomped my foot. "Darn it!" I cried spunkily. "Why do they have so many kids? Every time I come to stay with you they have another baby." I presume I remember this because I heard my grandfather tell it so often—chuckling as he did so.

This gentleman may have had his faults—visible to an adult's eye, but never to a child. He was a rolling stone. He gathered little moss; it was friends that he gathered. He never remained in one place long enough to reap the benefits of a good friendship.

Unhappily, like Paul, he had a thorn in his side. Pricking him often, but never hard—this was my grandmother.[2] Oh please! Don't misunderstand me. She was a good woman. Maybe even "gooder", as the children might say, when it came right down to solid virtues, than he was, but you'd never make me believe it.

But she was all business, never much for levity. I'm sure all her life her husband's fun-loving qualities—that so delighted others—irked her. She was the sort, too, who would have preferred to stay in one place and put down roots. Perhaps she believed that riches came only to those that settled down. Not that she especially wanted the things that money could buy. It was the status that came with wealth that she coveted. While she was by no means the kowtowing kind, she looked up to people with money.

Oh, my grandfather made money, a good deal with hotels, but he seemed unable to hold on to it. As one of his daughters told me, "Father had good judgment. He bought some good farms in his time, but he was never able to hold on to them until they brought him a profit. Farms he lost later brought their buyers good money."

How did my grandparents ever meet? I'll tell you! He, born on a farm near Plymouth, Vermont, the distant relative and neighbor of a man later to become President;[3] she, the daughter of a wealthy farmer in Michigan.

When Grandfather's widowed mother remarried,[4] he worked his way west as a brakeman on the new railroad, to live with an uncle in Kalamazoo. There he went to work for a farmer, fell in love with, and married his daughter, where upon the bride's father

3

gave him a farm. How they eventually got from that farm into the hotel business, I don't know.[5]

One of his first ventures was a new hotel, The Cook House,[6] in Rochester Minnesota, where my father attended school with the famous Mayo's.

Though I was born in a Minneapolis hotel[7] which my grandparents ran, my first memories of them are in a hotel in the small town of Fort Dodge, Iowa.[8]

Though Grandfather was a hotel man by trade, he remained a farmer at heart, and whenever he had a hotel, nearby he had a farm where he kept horses. My earliest memories of him are also associated with those horses.

I remember sitting beside my grandmother one day, eating an orange, when Grandfather came to the door of her room to tell me to come into the hall, he had something to show me. It was a long, wide, sumptuous-looking hall with wall to wall carpeting, oil paintings on the wall, a massive walnut table flanked by two heavy, high-backed walnut chairs. It was most regal.

Not a place for a horse under any circumstances, but that's what I saw when I entered. A beautiful little black Shetland pony stood there! And while I gasped, my grandfather set me on its back and "rode" me up and down the hall, from the grinning porter at one end to my astounded and disapproving grandmother at the other. Alice going through the looking glass could have been no more bewildered nor happier than I.

Alas! My delight was cut short. For that dear little pony wasn't housebroken and while Grandfather stood helpless, and Grandmother horrified, he did what no self-respecting pony should ever do on a red velvet carpet. Then Grandmother, stiffening into action, sent the porter-no longer grinning- for a broom and dustpan. She ordered Grandfather down the red-carpeted stairs up which he and his charge had ascended so happily. Grandfather had bought that pony for me, but my father, not one to fuss over either children or animals as his father did, vetoed my having it.

Another picture that comes to mind is of my grandfather and myself, a child of about eight years then, riding in a sulky, around the streets of Minneapolis, pulled by a spirited race horse that Grandfather was training. Sometimes Grandfather would let me hold the lines and pretend I was driving. But that wasn't exciting enough for me. One day I began teasing him to let me drive the horse, all alone. Well, you wouldn't think he would, would you? But, he did.

I could wheedle Grandfather into anything. "But just one block," he cautioned, standing beside the sulky, handing  over the reins. "And don't go along the streetcar tracks."

But that's exactly where I went. Along the streetcar tracks. Not that I meant to. But I missed the first turn I should have made, and along the next street ran the streetcar tracks. Fortunately, no street cars came as I traveled it, and I reached my grandfather, who was beginning to worry about my delay, without mishap.

Unfortunately, something worse than the coming of a street car happened. Grandmother caught us. She happened to glance out the window just as I drove up and Grandfather lifted me from the sulky. I can still hear her furious, incredulous, "Carl Merrill, do you mean you let that child...!"

Poor Grandmother! If only she could have known how often she took the joy out of Grandfather's life, and mine! Grandfather, always so meek, was like a small boy who'd done wrong and knew he must take his punishment. But, fortunately, he was also like a cork in a tub of water. Push it down and it would bob right back up. Grandfather would soon be bubbling again.

One hotel, then another! I have no idea how it happened that for a few years my grandparents lived on a farm in southern Iowa,9 but the memories of my visits there are still a part of me. I remember the homesickness that came over me when Grandmother lighted the lamps at night – loneliness for my mother, brothers, and sisters. But I loved my summers on that farm, the entirely different experiences – the freedom! There was scarcely a "don't" to govern me and there were big barns, the pigs, horses, the big grove of tall slim trees back of the house where I played, the small tent that Grandfather pitched there for me to play in.

But I loved best to trail after Grandfather, watching all the exciting things he did. There was the day he took me to see the litter of pretty little pigs that the big white sow just farrowed.[10] I had to stand on the lower rail of the fence to peek over the top of the pen to see them. Instantly I loved those baby pigs and begged my grandfather to let me hold one. So he reached down, lifted one up and put it into my arms.

He left me there, still holding it. Maybe I held too tightly. Suddenly it let out a squeal that not only scared the wits out of me but brought the old sow crashing across the pen and right into the fence. I'm sure nothing ever left my hands so quickly as that baby pig. I flung it back over the fence. For just an instant I saw it lying on the ground as if dead. Convinced I had killed it, I ran to my Grandmother.

I didn't tell her what happened. All day long, every time I saw my grandfather coming to the house, I trembled, thinking he was coming to tell me the little pig had died and perhaps punish me. But the little pig was pluckier than I thought; evidently he survived, and nothing happened to me.

Another memory that stands out as clearly as any that happened while I was on that farm is of an evening when my grandparents and the hired man stood at the foot of the stoop, looking off toward the horizon, talking in muted tones, while I stood, a shivering mite, beside them. There was something eerie in the air. It was growing dark. A peculiar light shone in the sky. I heard the words prairie fire.

What a prairie fire might be I had no idea. From the solemn tones of the men I knew it must be something to be afraid of, and my childish fear conjured up the memory of an Elk's parade I'd once seen in Minneapolis, headed by a huge and hideous dragon that kept turning its head from side to side, belching fire, as it dragged its length along the street. Certainly a prairie fire must be a beast of some kind.

Eventually we went into the house and to bed. But no sleep for me! I kept seeing some fiery animal racing across the field, burning us alive. But suddenly I remembered the new leather tam-o-shanter that my grandmother had just bought me and I'd left in the tent. I dearly loved that cap. Fear that it might be burned to nothing got me out of bed, and sent me hurrying down the hall to my Grandparent's room.

Now my grandmother was no woman to crawl out of bed to rescue a small cap. But assuring me that nothing would harm my cap, gently she drew me into bed with them. But it was my grandfather, who, as I sank deep into the feather bed between them, talked to me till I went to sleep.

I can wish no little girl on earth anything better that to have a grandfather like mine. God bless him! I'm sure that my love of fun and jokes, which so often distresses my family, is a direct heritage from him. It is a good legacy!

MY GRANDMOTHER'S KITCHEN

My childhood memories are filled almost as much with my paternal grandparents as with those of my parents, for I was with them so often. Not only because they dearly loved me, but because my mother was so busy having babies (eventually there were twelve of us) that she was glad to occasionally loan out the eldest, who was me.

Among my happiest memories are those of the times I spent with them on a small Iowa farm. How they came to be farming at their age, their children married with children of their own, I've often wondered. For Grandfather, though born on a Vermont farm, was a hotel man. But when he was on this farm, there was no hotel in the offing.

My grandmother was a tall, raw-boned woman, and I remember her always – except when she went to town – in long, drab, grey calico wrappers which hung loosely from a yoke and were finished off at the bottom with a ruffle – a garb worn by most women of that era.

She was a stern woman, who'd put up with no nonsense, but she was always kind and gentle with me, and I know that she loved to have me with her, pattering around after her, chattering, as she went about her work. But her tongue when she spoke to Grandfather, or to anyone of whom she disapproved, could often be sharp.

Except for the kitchen, it was a cold house, lacking all those little touches that turn a house into a home. I can still see it as clearly as if I'd just walked out of it. The door to the parlor, down the hall, a little way off the kitchen , was kept closed. But who would want to open it? The room had a stiff, unrelenting look. Every rocker set just so! In the center a square table holding the big family Bible, set precisely on a crocheted doily. The room bristled with varnish and cleanliness. I don't recall the room ever being used except when the minister called.

Upstairs, reached by a steep, tortuous stairway which opened into a large hall, were two bedrooms. One in which my grandparent's slept; the other the "hired man's room." My bed with its huge featherbed which seemed to enfold me when I crawled into it, was in the hall. Also here was a large heating stove, beside it a basket of wood and a sack of hickory nuts, the latter gathered from the hickory grove behind the house, in which I played.

But Grandmother's kitchen – ah, that was a different matter! An oasis in a desert. It was a long, wide room with a bay window at one end, with a window seat on which I used to play or look at picture books. The board floor, kept spotless by Grandmother's scrub brush, was covered with a scattering of home-made rugs. Nothing needless was here either, unless it was the gay pillow in the Boston rocker or on the window seat. But this room had a warm, cozy feeling, for here all our living was done.

At one side stood the big, always shiny, black range with its bulging warming oven, hot water reservoir at one end, beside it a never empty woodbox. Across the room was the sink. Boarded up below, here Grandmother kept her skillets and kettles, all smokey-bottomed from being set directly over the open fire.

The pump at one end of the sink gave only cistern water. Water for drinking and cooking came from an outside pump a few steps from the back door. A pail of drinking water with a long handled dipper from which everyone drank, dropping it back into the pail, stood on a nearby table.

At the opposite end of the kitchen from the bay window stood the long dining table, always set. For after Grandmother had done the dishes she reset the table, ready for the next meal. In the middle of the table stood a pewter cruet with its condiments, the covered cracker and sugar bowls, spoon holder, and salt and peppers. Over all this between meals was spread a long cheese cloth cover, hemstitched in bright colors around the edge. It was an arrangement found in all homes of that era.

There were always extra chairs for any unexpected guests who might happen in. For in horse and buggy days, with farms miles apart, the next town hours away, anyone appearing at mealtime was fed and, often, "slept."

The peddler with his pots, pans and other household needs, being a dubious character of doubtful cleanliness and weird appearance, was required to sleep in the hayloft. For this privilege he presented his hostess, on leaving, with a shiny stew pot, a box of thread, or perhaps if he really "took" to her, a more personal gift – a scarf or silken ribbon.

The Boston rocker was often occupied by Grandmother's cat curled up cozily asleep. Grandmother would never disturb it. She'd take a straight chair instead. However, Grandfather felt no qualms about removing the cat when he wanted to sit there!

I loved to stand beside the table under the pantry window and watch Grandmother knead her bread, mix her cakes or biscuits, or roll out cookies, on top of which she'd let me sprinkle the sugar. It was an oblong room, made quite narrow by shelves on either side where she kept her dishes. On one wider shelf stood a long row of large round milk pans which every night Grandfather would fill with milk after he'd milk the cows. When the cream had risen, Grandmother would skim it off – thick, leathery, cream-colored layers – and dump it into a crock to ripen for churning. The skimmed milk she would pour back into the big milk cans for Grandfather to carry out to the hogs.

I liked to watch Grandmother churn too. She'd sit in a straight chair, the wooden churn held firmly between her knees, and as she worked the wooden plunger up and down, we'd visit.   About sensible things. What made cream rise? Why some "cows" gave milk and others – like the bull – gave none. And maybe I'd beg her, "Tell me again, Grandma, about the time the horse kicked Papa and made a big hole in his head, and you sewed him up."

So she'd tell me how my father, when a little boy, had been teasing the new colt and its mother got mad and kicked, cutting a deep gash in his forehead, leaving a scar he wore all his life. As they lived too far from a doctor, Grandmother, with darning needle and heavy thread, had drawn the wound together, taking seven stitches. "Didn't he cry?" I always wanted to know. "Didn't it hurt him?"

Finally, a certain splashy sound, unmistakable to the initiated, would tell her the butter had come. Then she'd set the churn upon a chair, draw off the thick, rich buttermilk, flecked with tiny specks of butter, from a spigot in the bottom. Next she'd gather the butter together, transfer it to a large wooden bowl, wash it in several waters, and work it with a wooden paddle until not a drop of water could be squeezed out.

She'd then pack it in small crocks, or mold it into one pound bars, to be taken to town with her eggs and dressed chickens on market day, where she'd exchange it all for groceries, or anything else needed on the farm. It never dawned on me, watching her, that some fifteen or twenty years later, I'd marry a farmer and do almost the identical things. Only instead of delivering my produce behind a team of frisky horses, I'd be taking mine to market in a nifty Model T Ford!

Sometimes in the evening Grandmother would bring down a pan of hickory nuts from the upstairs hall, and with an old sad iron held upside down firmly between her knees, she'd crack the nuts with a hammer and drop them into a bowl for me to pick out the meats. Sometimes the meats were just to eat, or maybe we'd save enough for a cake, or hermits, which she'd let me drop by spoonfuls on greased cookie pans. That's when I liked Grandmother's kitchen best, when I could help her bake.

I helped her hang things on the line too. Handing them to her out of the clothes basket. She didn't have a washing machine. Nobody did. She scrubbed things on a washboard in a tub set on a bench or old backless chair. I can still see her bending over that tub, pushing Grandfather's shirts, or overalls, up and down, on that corrugated zinc washboard. Washing must have taken her a long time!

Those were happy times. During the day I'd go tagging along at the farm after Grandfather. I'd watch him feed the pigs, throw hay from the mow for the horses, or ride with him on the high seat of a rattley lumber wagon.

The only time I got homesick was at dusk when Grandmother started lighting the lamps. One on the warming oven of the stove, another on the bracket by the mirror over the sink where the men washed up and combed their hair, scrouching down a little to see better.

The larger lamp in the middle of the table that spread a circle of light over the checkered cloth and over our plates. The homesickness would rush in. Everything was so still, and I'd think of my brothers and sisters having fun at home, and of my mother, and it would be hard to hold back the tears.

Grandmother, sensing this, would have me do little things to help get supper. The men would come in, noisily, and wash up. Night would drop a protective darkness around the house and the lamps would push the shadows back into the corners of the room. Sitting beside Grandmother, listening to the men laugh and joke as they ate, I'd forget home, and be happy to be just where I was, in Grandmother's kitchen.

HOME IS A HOTEL!

Doubtless the affection between my grandparents and me stemmed not alone from the fact that I was a first grandchild, but that, born in their Minneapolis hotel, I lived with them for over a year.

How did this happen? My father was Grandfather's day clerk, so naturally lived in the hotel. When I was little more than a year old, Grandfather learned that a hotel in Ft. Dodge Iowa, The Duncombe House, was seeking a buyer. [11]

As this was pioneer country, with homesteaders, prospectors, and adventurers streaming in to get a foothold in this new land, always one to believe that the grass on the other side of the fence was more succulent, Grandfather decided to move there.

So we moved with them. But my mother was too spirited a woman to submit long to the domination of so inflexible a woman as my Grandmother. So when she heard of a new hotel in a nearby town seeking a manager, she persuaded my father to apply for the job. Which he did, and got it. He wasn't the manager long; with the town inundated with people seeking to get started in this new territory, Dad found the hotel so profitable he decided to buy it.

Here again Mother came to his assistance. One of the stockholders whom Mother had met was a pleasant German gentleman with a wife equally delightful. Both plump, short, and jolly, they might have stepped right out of a fairytale. Not long from Germany, they spoke English hesitantly. Mother, born of German immigrant parents[10] who had eloped and come to Iowa, got along with them famously. In fact, Mrs. Brennecke thought so much of Mother that she was instrumental in persuading the stockholders, through her husband, to let Dad, who had little money at the time, buy the hotel. And that's how it happened that I grew up in a hotel in Webster City, Iowa – a small town which, like a newborn colt, was struggling to its feet.

The hotel was an imposing large square brick building which, including the basement, stood four

stories high. It was surrounded on two sides by a wide covered porch, furnished with comfortable arm and rocking chairs.

Here, on warm summer evenings, the drummers (the transient salesmen to whom the hotel catered) might sit, feet on the porch rail, smoking pipes or cigars – never cigarettes – watching the girls go by. The town girls were well aware of this surveillance. Dressed in their best, they'd stroll slowly back and forth in front of the hotel, hoping a date might ensue, as it often did.

My mother, too, with some of her friends, used to sit there on pleasant evenings, with us children playing around them. It was a sort of family porch, for many of the traveling men came so regularly that we came to know them as friends. In fact, the lovely thing about that town, and that hotel, was that everyone knew and were friends to everyone else.

Around the hotel ran a boardwalk, set a foot or so above the ground, and made of narrow boards, laid on the bias, with wide cracks between. Should a child drop a penny, or a nickel – big money in those days – she could crawl under the walk to retrieve it. An unpleasant task in muddy weather, as I can well testify, but should she find a coin or two that some other unfortunate had lost, the effort was well worth it.

The roads on both sides of the hotel were dirt, wide, and dusty often to suffocation in Iowa's hot  and muggy summers. In spring or rainy weather they could turn to mud in which a vehicle with wheels could easily sink. Although we moved to the hotel in the early nineties, it was not until 1909 that the roads were paved with bricks.

From the porch, double doors opened into a dark and gloomy hall from which rose a red carpeted stairway to the bedrooms. To the left of the hall was a large writing room, provided with a long desk topped with a full-length mirror. Here the drummers made out their days orders, or wrote home to their wives. Here also was a shoe shine chair, staffed by either porter or yardman, depending on which one was free at the time.

To the right of the hall, a door opened into an office, made as dark and gloomy as the hall by the overhanging porch. One end of the room was cut off by a long desk on which sat the cash register and the hotel ledger in which the transients signed in.

From the rear of the dark hall opened a large and cheery dining room, where nine tables, invitingly set with spotless damask table linen and glistening silver, would each seat six or eight guests, as necessity demanded. By day the room was lighted by long deep-silled windows on opposite sides of the room. Oil lamps, that had to be cleaned daily, were set in brackets between each window and lighted the room at night. In summer, shades were drawn to darken the room between meals and sticky fly papers were laid around on tables and windowsills. By night, they were black with their catch of flies.

Off from the dining room was the kitchen. This large room was divided into two sections. One section housed the pantry cook, the dishwashers, and the girl who washed the silver. The other section contained the big black range and the steam table. Here were prepared the many dishes offered on my father's menu. This part of the kitchen also held two walk-in iceboxes in which the food was kept fresh. The first icebox was used for storing fruits and vegetables, and the second, directly behind the first, was where all the meat was stored.

The hotel had fifty rooms, but no number thirteen. Who, in that superstitious age, would have slept in it? Fifty rooms – a few of which were occupied by help or regular boarders – and not a single bathroom! Each room was supplied with a commode on which set a bowl and pitcher, soap dish, and mug. Underneath was an article bearing the obnoxious name of "slop jar." Other toilet facilities were in a long wooden building behind the hotel and connected to it by a wide boardwalk which ran along the outside and back of the second floor.

Eventually our large windowless linen closet was converted into a bathroom. A large box near the ceiling provided water released for flushing by the pull of a chain. When a new addition was added to the hotel, four rooms were furnished with private bathrooms.

The upstairs parlor was perhaps the nicest room in the hotel; to my childish eyes it was a place of grandeur. Satin upholstered furniture, lovely lace curtains, a piano, and in one corner of the room an article of furniture that much resembled a cupboard with an elegant fringed chenille covering. A large crayon picture of myself, my hair in becoming curls, was hung on the wall over the piano.

The piano I remember especially because I had to spend so much time there (that I'd much have preferred to spend somewhere else!) practicing. I had to practice piano for one half hour every day. I can well remember getting up from the bench and calling down the hall to my mother, "Is my half hour up yet?" I must have spent half my practice time doing that! Mother, growing impatient, would often threaten me that if I called once more, I'd have to practice double my time.

The choice times with that piano would be when some traveling man with itchy fingers would sit down and pound out melodies that would make your feet dance! Other guests, if it were evening, would either come in and listen to the concert, or enjoy the music from the wide hall outside the parlor.

My best friend, Junie,[12] and I, inspired by the many stock company shows that we attended at the local opera house, would use the parlor to "play show." We'd reenact wonderful dramas that we'd seen. Once our zeal was so great that we were standing on those beautiful upholstered chairs, acting our little hearts out. My father happened by and immediately gave us a stiff lecture about not standing on the furniture.

There was, however, a higher authority than Dad. One Sunday when we were engaged in play acting there came a terrific thunder storm. It grew almost as dark as night, thunder roared, lightening flashed, rain beat against the window, the wind blew. From the window we could see wind-propelled articles flying down the street. Saying we were frightened is putting it mildly! We thought it must be a cyclone, a much dreaded disaster that often destroyed whole towns in Iowa.

But we really believed was that God was doing this to punish us for playing show on Sunday. With all seriousness we got down on our knees and promised God that if he'd make the storm stop, we'd never play show again on Sunday. Sunday was a sacred day then. Our mothers forbid us to do many things on Sunday. One of my friend's mother refused to let us play paper dolls. Instead we were told to go for a walk. That occupation could have gotten us into a lot more mischief than mere paper dolls, for generally we'd meet up with some boys and spend our afternoon with them. Had my friend's mother ever learned about that, it would surely have been on her list of taboos!

One thing we were not allowed to do was sew on Sunday, and what more innocent occupation could there have been than that? We were told that when we went to heaven, every stitch we had taken on Sunday we'd have to take out with our nose! Ridiculous as that sounds, it was firmly believed. However, as I disliked sewing at any time, that rule didn't bother me in the least!

In the twinkling of an eye, that wonderful parlor could be converted into a bedroom. When we had more guests than rooms, the parlor would be called into service. The top of the table, which was on hinges, would be raised, displaying a mirror on its underside. The inside contained a bowl and pitcher, soap dish, mug, and that inevitable slop jar. The front of the mirror cabinet in the corner pulled down to reveal a bed, all nicely made, and ready for occupancy for two, if any two sleepy transients cared to share it.

Sometimes, if the hotel was overflowing with guests, I'd have to give up my room. One morning, after such a sacrifice, I returned to my room and found four boxes of candy on my dresser. Evidently, the occupant had been a candy salesman and as a courtesy had left me a gift!

One incident that happened in the parlor should of shattered my childish ego. It didn't, of course! One day Mother was showing a woman through the hotel, and I, in pigtails and rumpled play clothes, was tagging along. Mother was displaying the parlor with great pride, but her guest's attention was suddenly riveted on my picture over the piano. "My!" She exclaimed. "What a beautiful child!"

Mother puffed up, and nodding toward me with pride explained, "That's Irene." Evidently the woman didn't quite see eye to eye with Mother. For after a long and far from admiring look at me, she said, "My, how she has changed!"

Our whole hotel had wall to wall carpeting, the hallways in deep red. Unlike hotels of today, whose rooms are not only closed but locked, our hotel room doors were left wide open, allowing a good view of the immaculateness within.

Though most of the hotel must have been lighted at first with lamps, I remember none except those in the dining room and in Mother's suite. She had a very beautiful table lamp with a round floral globe and a base to match. Also a floor or piano lamp, so called because it could be moved so that anyone playing a piano could read the music. A common oil lamp, which stood on Mother's bedroom dresser, did double duty as she used it to heat the iron with which she curled her – and often my – hair.

Later the hotel was piped for gas, which was a little improvement as far as light was concerned, but which did have the advantage of not needing daily attendance. Pipes, with a "jet" at the end, stuck out from the wall. When one turned a knob and held a match to the jet, a yellowish-blue light sprang into being. Eventually, an article, a small bag called a mantle, was invented which, tied to the jet, gave a diffused and much better light. But, once lighted, the mantles were so fragile that the slightest puff of wind would shatter them. Hence, they were used only in the most important places, such as the office, dining room, and Mother's rooms. When electricity was finally installed, this ended the light, and even many work, problems.

The basement of our hotel contained our laundry, comprised of three rooms. In the first room linens were put in a big barrel-like machine that, lacking electricity, had to be turned by hand. The machine had corrugated walls inside. After washing, the clothes were run through a wringer by hand. The wash was then dried in a second room, on racks heated by pipes from a coal stove.

In the third room, which was light and cheery, all the dampened sheets were put in a heavy wooden press, at one time, and it was screwed down tight. Even though there was no heat, when the sheets were removed, several hours later, they were as smooth as if hand-ironed. Table linens and pillowcases, however, were ironed by hand using heavy triangle irons heated on a small coal stove.

Eventually a cold mangle was added to the laundry equipment. Comprised of two heavy rollers turned by a hand crank, it ironed table linens, towels, and pillowcases beautifully, surprising the skeptics who had said it couldn't be done without heat.

In the basement was a barber shop, its striped pole informing the unshaven that here they could get a "shave and a hair cut, two bits." Next door was a "sample room" provided with long wide tables on which drummers could display their wares for local merchants who would come and place their orders.

Here, too, was a large room, its darkness from the porch outside held at bay by oil lamps, provided with two pool tables. At election time it served also as a polls. Voting booths were set up and at night political rallies were held. What excitement then when campaigning men and their followers (no women!) went marching down the street, their smoking torches lighting up the night, the band behind them playing, "There'll be a Hot Time in the Old Town Tonight." Let no one think so young a town lacked in ardor when it came to politics.

The charge for one day's luxuries at my father's hotel was two dollars. Fifty cents a room, the same for each meal. The menu listed no prices.

The whole caboodle could be had for one fifty cent piece. At least four meats were offered and a diner could order all four if he wished. In all the years my father ran the hotel those prices never changed.

THE WILLSON

W. N. MERRILL, Prop.

Christmas Dinner, A. D. 1912

Oyster Cocktail

Mulligatawney   Consomme Royal

Celery   Olives   Radishes   Sliced Cucumbers

Mexican Chili Con Carne

Boiled Sugar Cured Ham—Champagne Sauce
Candied Sweet Potatoes

Emince of Chicken—a la Prett

Prime Ribs of Beef—au jus   Roast Young Turkey—Oyster Dressing
Mashed Potatoes   Cranberry Sauce

Peach Compote with Fruited Rice

Patties of Calf Brains   French Peas

Braised Domestic Duck—Apple Sauce
Spinach   Mock Chestnut Dressing
Lobster en Mayonnaise

Apple Pie   Pumpkin Pie   Mince Pie

American Cheese   Salted Wafers

English Plum Pudding—Hard Sauce

Chocolate Ice Cream   Assorted Cake

Mixed Nuts   Fruit   Sweet Cider

Coffee   Tea   Cocoa   Milk

50¢

HELPING HANDS

With a few exceptions, our help seemed like part of our family. An amiable and trusting association. Though they stood somewhat in awe of my father, they were very fond of my mother and she had a real affection for most of them. Perhaps because she would pitch in and help wherever she was needed.

Most of our girls came from surrounding small towns or farms. Wanting to escape farm drudgery, as farm life then often was, they probably hoped for an easier, more exciting life.[13]

Certainly it was not the wages that attracted them. Three of our dining room girls were paid eighteen dollars a month. Yes! A month! The headwaitress, who had full responsibility of the dining room, received $20. In off hours, two of the dining room girls doubled as chambermaids. The third was the "silver girl." She washed and cared for the glass and silverware. Butter was also her responsibility. I liked to watch her make butter patties, with a wooden mold that had a print on top. The patties, served on small white china butter chips, were three or four times the size of the almost invisible slice one is served today. There was no custom of compulsory tipping in those days. If perchance a man might leave a dime beside his plate, for a girl he liked, she'd hold it out in her extended palm, as if it were a silver dollar, boasting, "See what I got."

Any of us girls, when we were old enough, could work for Dad for pay. It certainly wasn't required of us; the choice was ours. One or two of my sisters did. They liked the extra spending money. Not I! Whenever possible, I always took the easy path. I got my food and clothes. For spending money I used what I could cajole from Mother. You see, I was no admirable character!

Often our chef and second cook were a married couple, and I doubt that we ever had a couple that didn't drink and consequently fight. Often I would hear one couple, whose room was above Mother's, throwing things at each other. Once it was an alarm clock. I knew, because it started ringing when it hit the floor.

The trouble with hiring couples was that when one quit, so did the other. Then Dad would have to contact an employment agency in Minneapolis for reinforcements. In the meantime, Mother, aided by the "black" dishwasher, would have to carry on. And don't think she couldn't. Though it was hard for her, with the children to care for, often she did a better job than a professional

Dick[14] was a good chef. He had a knack for cooking. Everybody who worked with him liked him. He was quiet, pleasant, courteous, and a bachelor! When he was in the kitchen everything went smoothly. My mother was very fond of him. Though he was in his late twenties or early thirties, Mother spoke of him as "a good boy."

Unfortunately, he was an alcoholic. Every so often he'd go off on a binge. Then the second cook, and dishwasher, and perhaps Mother, would have to take over. But, because he was faithful, and so good when sober, my parents never fired him.

A girl came into Dick's life; unfortunately, she was the wrong kind. Her mother, a large, heavy-set, unpleasant woman, was the second cook. The red-haired daughter was not a particularly pleasant person either, nor was she attractive. Her very light blue eyes detracted from her appearance.

But somehow she got a hold on Dick. I don't think their affair was initiated by him. She roomed with her mother, but after everyone was in bed, she'd slip into Dick's room and spend the night. In those days, nothing was more degrading to a girl's reputation than that. Yet somehow, although everyone knew what was going on, they closed their eyes or looked the other way. The affair finally ended when the girl and her mother left. Dick stayed on.

Of the many pastry cooks we must have had, I remember only two. One, a tall, thin woman, who talked little, was very efficient. She had a small daughter who, while her mother beat up cakes or rolled out pie crust, played quietly nearby with her dolls. I felt something sad about the woman. She was a loner. Aloof! Once her work was done, she went up to her room.

The other one I remember because she talked TOO much – and always about her ailments. She spent most of her time sitting in a chair, spooning medicine from a bottle. Her worst fault was drinking; but she never indulged so much that she couldn't do her work. She didn't stay with us long.

Between pastry cooks Mother was often called upon to fill in. She preferred this job to that of being one of the main cooks. She liked to bake good cakes, pies, and puddings, and prepare the salads, which was part of the pastry cook's job. One of our regular boarders once remarked that he could always tell when Mrs. Merrill was in the kitchen, the salads were so good. Mother once said if she HAD to earn her living, she wouldn't mind being a pastry cook.

The thing she disliked about these cooking jobs was that she always had to have one of the help take care of the baby. For, with a child born every two years, there was always a baby in the family. One hot day, after her work was done and she wearily climbed the stairs and opened the door to her room, she found the baby sitter reading a novel, while in the carriage the baby screamed her lungs out, her head covered with a blanket to smother the sound. Needless to say, this girl was NOT treated as one of the family! She was promptly fired.

Tillie![15] Goodness, I must not forget Tillie. Of all the help we ever had she was among the most faithful. She was a laundry girl from before I remember until after I was married. A tall woman, she was without an ounce of charm. She dressed in drab clothes, wore her hair in a straggly bun, and was set in her ways as cement. Once she made up her mind, God himself couldn't budge her. But Mother thought a lot of Tillie.

So did I. I used to go down to the laundry to "help" her fold the sheets to put in a press, then help screw it down tight. Tillie would iron the pillowcases, towels, and table linens, but sometimes she would let me iron the napkins. Although the irons were heavy for me to carry from the stove, she insisted that if I were big enough to iron I'd have to carry my own. Once, when I had just changed from cold to hot iron, the strong smell of burning cloth polluted the air.

"Irene!" Tillie cried. "You're burning your dress." True enough! I'd held the iron too close to my skirt. But I shrugged away the tragedy with a nonchalant, "It doesn't matter. My mother's having a new dress made for me and it'll soon be done." I imagine my mother didn't share my opinion!

If one of the chambermaids conked out, my services might be needed. Then Tillie would come up to make sure I did my job right. Bottom sheets – no fitted sheets then – had to be stretched tight, top sheets turned back, once and then again, leaving half the sheets exposed. When it came to such things, Tillie was a martinet.[16] Once she caught me dusting with a towel and jumped all over me. Didn't I know that dirt ground into towels was difficult to get out? Bed-making I didn't mind. Waiting on table, I hated.

Regardless of her lack of charm, Tillie had a faithful beau, George,[17] our yardman. George courted her for years. He wanted to marry her, but she refused. They never went anyplace, doubtless because she wouldn't. She'd entertain him in her room. Always, however, with the door wide open. Someone was always asking her, "Tillie, why don't you <u>marry</u> George?" She'd never answer.

Tillie's parents had a good farm and money in the bank, though they acted as if the next nickel they spent would be their last. When Tillie's parents died within a short time of each other, Tillie quit us and went home to take care of her brother, left alone on the farm.

One day we were driving by her farm and dropped in to see her. She was picking corn, wearing overalls long before they were popular garb for women, but she came in the house to visit with us. We entered through the kitchen and never have I seen so dismal a room. Long,  windowless, and narrow, it might have once been a pantry. The walls were as black, from smoke, as the range she cooked on, and it was the only article of furniture in the room.

The living room was clean but cheerless. Egg crates or boxes were in every chair. She had to move them to find us a place to sit. A room unloved, unlived in! She seemed glad to see us, but acted as if she'd like to get back to work. She talked of getting the corn out before snow time. I left there depressed. Tillie, of whom my mother had been so fond, a wealthy woman, yet this was the way she chose to live. I doubt that she ever spent one cent unnecessarily while working for us.

I don't remember when Briget,[18] our "black" dishwasher, came to work for us. She was called black, not because of the color of her skin, but because of the black iron pots and pans she used to scrape, wash, and care for. A little old maid – as all unmarried girls over thirty were then called – her fate seemed doomed. I gave small thought to her plight, as a child, but have thought often of it since. What a cheerless life she must have led. At that sink, next to the hot stove, washing greasy pots and pans most of the day, other times preparing vegetables. How exhausted she must have been when finally, late at night, she climbed the two flights of back stairs to her cheerless room.

How she ever found time to find a husband, how she ever overcame her timidity and looked at a man, I wonder. She was Irish and a Catholic, and like a true Catholic she attended church regularly. Perhaps she found in God some compensation for her lonely life.

Perhaps here, too, she found her husband. Some man who saw shining good beneath her dull exterior. No one knew the man, only that he was a farmer of considerable means. Everyone was so happy for her, and hoped that the man would be good to her.

Especially my mother even though she was losing a faithful worker.

Though we knew that she moved to a nearby farm, we almost lost track of her. Then we learned that wonder of wonders, Briget was pregnant, but tragically her husband had a terminal illness. Now we hoped that the baby would be born before her husband died. Due to an Iowa law, we knew that if she had a child when her husband dies, her inheritance would be larger. So it happened, and Briget inherited the farm.

Odd how I remember some girls who worked for us, others not at all. The only dishwasher, besides Briget, that I remember was a woman who just wasn't "all there." She was short, uncouth, and dumpy. Yet when it came to mathematics, she was as sharp as a whip. Perhaps the reason she sticks in my mind is that on the Fourth of July, Circus days, or during any celebration when we fed large crowds, I often had to wipe dishes for her.

Much as I disliked that, I much preferred it to waiting table. I specifically remember one Fourth when I was asked to help out. It was during my convent school days when as a teenager my self-confidence was easily shattered. I got a table with eight young smart-alecks who had been drinking just enough to be silly. I took their orders; we never wrote them down but had to remember them. After I'd taken the last order, one fellow looked up at me and said with a silly grin, "Think you can remember that, Honey?"

I flew out into the kitchen and up the back stairs like a dog with its tail on fire. Confronting my mother angrily I said, "I hate waiting on table and I'm not going to do it." Then I told her what happened.

Generally when I didn't want to do a thing Mother took my side – as I expected her to do now. This time she had other ideas: "You march right back down into that dining room, young lady, and do what your father wants you to do. You've got to learn sometime that you can't always have your own way."

I was so surprised at this stand that I didn't even argue but did as she said. The blessing was that I'd been away long enough that someone else had attended to my table. I had no further difficulty that day.

Annie[19] was the head waitress I remember best of all. She came to work for us when I was very young and she remained with us for years. EVERYBODY liked Annie. Boarders, transients, the other girls. She was a large woman, not fat, and jolly, good-natured, generous. She'd do anything for anybody. She had a ready, infectious laugh. To mother she was the salt of the earth. She was with us until she married Bill,[20] our day clerk, and left to make a home for him.

Bill, a slight, pleasant, good looking young man was another who came to work for us before I can remember and was with us until he died. After his marriage to Annie he lived at his home, which was scarcely more than a block away, and he never missed a day of work. When I was little he used to let me sit with him at the big desk behind the counter and draw pictures.

His brother, Archie,[21] worked for us, too, as a porter, handy man, or whatever was needed. Perhaps I liked him best of all the boys or men who worked for us. Long before I was big enough to reach the footrest, he'd toss me up into the big shoe-shine chair and shine my tiny patent leather slippers. And as he buffed away, he'd tell me stories to make me laugh. Always a different story as to how he got his double thumbs.

For that was the unique thing about Archie; each of his thumbs ended in two thumbs, perfect in every detail. When I'd tell my schoolmates about Archie's thumbs, they wouldn't believe me or wanted to see for themselves. I'd bring them home with me and Archie, amused, would always put them on display.

Joe[22] was another who was always nice to us kids. He drove the bus to the depot to pick up the traveling salesmen and their luggage, then took them up to their rooms. Often he'd take me to the depot with him. Letting me sit right on the seat beside him. I loved the excitement of the station, watching the trains come in. Joe's job, too, was to go from room to room in late afternoon to fill the water pitchers.

As I think back, wondering how best to describe him, it strikes me that he was an English Cockney. Short, quick-moving, a bit plump, no other words seem to describe him as well. Another of Mother's favorites, he was with us for years.

Such a nice man to come to such an unhappy end. He had two faults that led to his undoing. Gambling, and though married, women. I'm sure he must have lost more betting than he could afford. He'd never miss a horse race if there were a way to get to it. But regardless of where he went at night, he always showed up for work each morning.

That's why Dad was so worried when he failed to show up one morning. Inquiries brought no information. No one knew where he'd gone. Sometime later the police brought the news; his body had been found under a bridge at the edge of a river. His clothes were bloody, but there was no sign of a wound. The undertakers, however, discovered that he'd been shot in the back. Where he had been, who shot him, and how he got under the bridge was never learned. I was old enough then not only to mourn for Joe, but to feel sorrow for his wife and three little girls.

George, Tillie's beau, and another of my favorites, was with us for years and years. A big, somewhat clumsy man, he was always on hand when needed. His jobs as "yardman" were varied. Taking care of the furnace in winter, doing certain things about the kitchen, taking care of the bus and baggage horses. It was here that I remember him best because I used to go down and watch him curry the horses, pestering him all the while with questions.

Peddlers and itinerant salesmen were also a part of hotel and town life. The ice wagon, the bakery wagon, horse-drawn vehicles that went up and down the street clanging their bells and women rushing out to buy from them. The chestnut vendor, horse-radish vendor, scissors grinder who carried his heavy equipment on his back.

Even the traveling tramps who came to back doors begging handouts, often offering to work for food. These men were part of the lifeblood of the town.

The barber shop men, Magg and Clifton, didn't work for us, but they were part of my young life. Their shop was in our basement –a big, well-lighted, and cheerful room, with three barber chairs and a wall of mirrors. I used to go down and read the jokes in Judge, Life, Punch, three magazines long defunct, they had for the convenience of waiting customers. I would sit quietly in one of their chairs while they trimmed my hair and joked with me. In the mirror I could see behind me the wall of small cubby holes in which the mugs and shaving brushes of their regular customers were kept – a name on each mug. I've often wished I had my father's mug.

Faithful as I have pictured the help to be, at one time all but one girl went on strike. This was very early in the hotel days when I was too young to remember. To get an entire staff immediately was impossible. To shut down was something my father would not do. What then? With a houseful of guests and regular borders, all my mother's friends came to the rescue. They donned their work clothes, tied aprons around their waists, and cooked, made beds, washed dishes, waited on table, everything, until a new crew was assembled. From all I've heard about it, her friends had a great time!

I've never known why the help struck. Some of the strikers wanted to come back, but Dad wouldn't take them. The girl who didn't strike was rewarded handsomely. The regular boarders and some of our regular transients made up a substantial purse and presented it to her.

In thinking back about the help, I am humbled by their attitude toward the hotel. Although many of the tasks assigned them were menial, they did their jobs cheerfully and were serious about their work. Certainly they made the hotel a special place for those of us who lived there and for the transients who, even for one night, could call it home.

MY PARENTS

To my childish eyes my parents were beautiful people. Happy, gay, -- when that word had a pleasanter meaning than it has today – they could also be serious. Light hearted, fun-loving, they were also ambitious, hardworking, as any young couple who had just bought a hotel had to be.

They made a good team; Dad attended to the financial end of the hotel, while Mother attended to its running. Born of German parents, my mother was a good worker. There was nothing that needed to be done that she wouldn't do. Kind, generous, helpful, tolerant, these were traits she had plenty of opportunity to use with the help they employed.

Dad was stern; when he spoke he expected to be obeyed, and always was. As with us children, the help stood a bit in awe of him. He could snap his fingers louder that anyone I knew, a sound that seemed to reverberate throughout the entire hotel. Should we be into mischief, the snap of those fingers would bring us quickly into line.

The help were very fond of my mother and would do almost anything she asked. With us children she was warm, loving, indulgent, and almost totally unable to discipline us, as she herself admitted. "I simply can't make that child mind!" How often have I heard her say that! As a consequence, knowing she'd given up before she started, it didn't take us kids long to learn that with Mother we could get away with anything.

Mother had one defense. When things got too rough, she'd threaten us, "I'll ring for your father." Which meant she'd ring for the porter, when he appeared she'd ask him to "please ask Mr. Merrill to step upstairs." She need go no further. The threat was enough. Quickly we'd assure her, "We'll be good, Mama." For our Father's punishment was drastic. Standing, he'd lift one knee, lay the culprit over it, and his hand, big enough to cover that entire part of the anatomy, would come down with all the force of a ten ton truck. To avoid this, we'd obey instantly.

My Mother was so beautiful that when she first came to our town and walked down the street, people turned to look after her. She had soft brown dark eyes, dark brown hair which to the end of her days she wore in a psyche knot on top of her head, with a soft roll of curls around her forehead. There was a radiance about her. She had a regal carriage. Fresh from Minneapolis, she knew how to dress.

Reason lay behind this. An expert seamstress, she had sewed in the homes of wealthy Minneapolis people. Doubtless here she had acquired her taste for beautiful clothes and her knowledge of how to wear them. Her dresses were mostly of silks, satins, velvets, often with a little train. As I first remember her, her dresses were made of a tight high-necked bodice, mutton-leg sleeves, her skirts enhanced by a bustle or pannier. Her corset, tightly drawn in, gave her that wasp-like figure so popular in that day. She never outgrew her love for beautiful clothes – both for herself and her many daughters.

I used to love to sit on Mother's bed and watch her curl her hair. She had a tin, doughnut-shaped contraption which she sat on top of her lamp chimney, in which she inserted her curling iron. She'd wet her finger and touch it to the iron to make sure it wasn't so hot it would burn her hair. Once her hair was properly done, she'd put on her hat, always small, before she donned her dress. For once she was buttoned into her tight bodice, she couldn't raise her arms to pin her hat in place.

My father was a tall, handsome man, and in his youth smartly dressed. His grey eyes, when amused, would break into a twinkle, a trait that increased as he aged and softened. But his eyes were generally stern. He had but to look at a child to make her behave. His hair when I first recall, was black, worn in a stiff, short pompadour. It whitened early, though he wore it the same. With white hair is how I best remember him.

I still see a guitar laying on my mother's living room lounge. I knew she took guitar lessons. I recall seeing her holding it once on her lap, twanging away, perhaps practicing, but that's the only time I remember her playing. She loved music, lively music. She was especially fond of Sousa, though she never heard his band until that old wind-up phonograph came into being. Did she yearn to make music of her own? If so, that yearning was buried in the rearing of a family.

I've so often thought of that. The cooing of babies, the laughter of children (also their crying and quarreling) became her music. That she did not have to make herself.

My parents had twelve children, each about two years apart, all born in Iowa but me. Eleven were born in her own bed, assisted by the same doctor. When she married, she said she wanted six boys, preferably in sets of twins. She felt girls were too hard to rear. One false step and their lives were ruined, which could be true in those days.

When I, her first, was born, she was disappointed. To console her my father took my small hand and said, "See those nice long piano fingers." Poor, misguided Dad! He paid for music lessons for me from my eighth to eighteenth year, and though I once received a certificate in music, I doubt that today I could play chopsticks.

Mother's second child was also a girl, but she died in infancy of pneumonia, then called lung fever. Today's greater knowledge and our magic medicines might have saved that baby girl. The remedy then was to keep the chest covered with hot flaxseed poultices.

To her great joy, Mother's third child was a son. She didn't know then that in his teens he would cause more trouble than all her daughters. Eventually, he developed into a fine young man of whom she was very proud. Altogether Mother had four boys. Two of them, who again might have been saved by today's knowledge, died in infancy. Seven girls and two boys managed to live to be sixty years or better. Beside their own children, my parents raised a niece[46] and a nephew, children of two of Mother's sisters who had died of consumption. Now known as TB, consumption then had no cure, and was as dreaded as cancer is today.

I have often thought of what a hard – but generally uncomplaining – life Mother led. Always a baby in her arms, and, as the saying went then, one under her apron. I think of the tremendous task of just keeping them clothed! Yet, no children had a better mother than did we kids. She nursed us all, except the last two perhaps; it seems I remember bottles. Afterwards, she rocked us in her arms, singing to us until we fell asleep – a valuable experience for a child. She'd sing us German songs that doubtless her mother sang to her. She also sang us songs from the Bohemian Girl. I remember "She's only a bird in a golden cage, a beautiful sight to see," and "I dreamed that I dwelt in marble halls."

Often we children would lean over the arm of her rocker, to peer into the face of the new baby as it nursed, and, as a consequence, getting too near her chair and getting our toes rocked on. "I've TOLD you to be careful," Mother would try to sooth us as we started to cry, "You must not get so near."

Mother would often have a hard time laying a sleeping baby back into her crib. For just as she'd be about to take her arms out from under her charge, one of us kids – or maybe all of us – would burst into the room with news to convey, and the baby would waken. Then Mother, who might want to get on to some other task, would throw her arms up in the air, crying out despairingly, "Can't you children EVER be quiet?"

Although Mother and Father had their hands full trying to raise a family and manage a hotel, they did try to keep up some sort of social life. They went to dances and parties. They used to let me go with them to the Elk's dances, an occasion I dearly loved. Sometimes I'd merely sit on the edge of the stage and watch the musicians play. Or, if other children were there, we might hop around the edge of the ballroom, imitating our elders.

I liked best to just sit, and watch my parents dance. Square dances, the Virginia reel, the Scottish or minuet. Mother always wore such beautiful dresses; they had long trains which she held over her arm when she danced. She always wore an ornament in her dark hair, a large fancy comb, or the delicate feathers of an egret – long before a law was passed that birds could not be killed to use on hair or hats.

My parents at one time belonged to a Whist²³ club and whenever the club met in our hotel parlor, I would be allowed to stay up a little while and watch. Mother didn't care for cards. She belonged to the group more for sociability, and because Dad wanted to. She had no card sense whatsoever, but she always held good hands and was lucky. So men liked her as a partner. Why not? She was a beautiful woman, pleasant and good-natured, and whoever played with her generally won.

All but my father. He, being sharp at cards himself, would get impatient with her hap-hazard playing. "What are you trying to do?" I once heard him say to her after the guests had left, "Take your aces home with you?"

Father liked best to play poker "with the boys." I remember his friends saying that to no one could the term "Poker faced" be applied better than to him.

Mother, not overly approving of the game, would go out and buy a piece of hand-painted china, (her weakness at the time) whenever she learned that he'd lost. As a result, we had some mighty pretty pieces of china about our house!

We received all our religious training from Mother, who was very devout. Once she prevailed upon Dad to go to church with her. Once there, everyone rushed to him with such warm and welcome greetings that he said he felt like the returned prodigal and never went again.

Father never gave us kids any parental advice in advance. If he wanted one of us to know something, what to do or how to behave, he'd go to Mother and tell her to tell us what he wanted us to know. Mother, always impatient with him for this, would say, "Will, if you want her to know that, you tell her." He never did. Only if we did something wrong did he have words for us.

Dad was a father of the old school. His idea was that running the hotel, being the provider, was his job. Mother's was rearing the children and with that he never helped her. I doubt if he'd have any idea of how to dress a child, even to buttoning her dress. As to diapering a baby, never in his life, to my knowledge, did he perform that operation. I can't even imagine him doing it. That was strictly out of his territory.

Dad's name was William Nicola Merrill. Most people called him Bill, but there were those who called him Pa Merrill, not an inappropriate moniker for one with so large a family.

Mother's name was Sophie. When he spoke to her directly, or of her to their friends, that's what he called her. To the help, she was always "The Missus." Dad's meal times were uncertain. He ate when he could leave the office. Then he'd ask whatever girl came to wait on him, "Will you please call the Missus?" She would call up the backstairs, and Mother would come down and join him. Though we had our own family table, except for certain holidays, we seldom ate together as a family. While the younger children would generally eat with our parents, we older kids would wander in whenever we pleased.

Having so large a family was not, I believe, exactly Mother's idea. Once when she was lamenting because she had learned she was to have a twelfth child, my father, taking a somewhat humorous means of consoling her said, "You wouldn't want people to think you were too old to have a baby, would you?" I have a notion Mother didn't fall in with that way of looking at the matter.

My brother, four years younger than I, must have felt somewhat as I did – or as I had expressed my feelings the day my grandfather read me the telegram informing me of a new sister. For one day when Mother was herding us to go shopping for school clothes and wanted him to go with us, Maris refused. "It looks like a Sunday school picnic," he said "and I don't want to get mixed up with it."

As it grew increasingly difficult to keep so many children quiet – crying, quarreling, or just laughing in good spirits – is was not unusual for the porter to come to Mother's room and when she answered his knock, say, "Mrs. Merrill, will you please try to keep the children quieter. People are complaining." Since transients were our livelihood and as such should have first consideration, Mother would struggle to tone us down and get us quietly to bed.

But on one occasion, my father was the disturber. He always stayed up to meet guests from the last train and get them bedded down before he came to bed, which was generally around one a.m. By then Mother would have long been asleep, the door locked. For the back stairs were directly opposite the door to our suite and my over-imaginative mother was fearful that someone might sneak up the back stairs and perhaps murder us. Generally Dad's knock would awaken her,

This night it didn't. After a long day's work, she was dead to the world. So Dad kept knocking softly, saying quietly, "Sophie wake up, let me in. Sophie wake up, let me in."

The softness that didn't waken Mother, had an adverse affect on the man across the hall for suddenly an angry voice roared out, "For God's sake, Sophie, wake up and let him in!" Is it necessary to add that after that, Dad always carried a key?

These are memories of my parents. Dad, running the hotel and thus unable to help Mother much with us, was a good provider and was always fair. And no woman could have been a better or more loving parent than our beautiful Mother. Unfortunately I, like many other children, realized their goodness and became appreciative years too late to pay them tribute. Their love and discipline kept me from many a possible disaster, and made me the reasonably good person I try to be.

HORSING AROUND

Horses were our main means of transportation when I was a child, and I have both pleasant and humorous memories of them. Even my accidents, as I look back on them, are laughable. One incident with my father I'll never forget.

Dad, like his father, had a yen for spirited horses. He had one team that he drove with a sporty one-seated runabout. The only time I recall riding in it was so unusual that no child could forget it.

The occasion was a visit from Cousin Ella[24] of Minneapolis, and my father took her for a ride to show her the wonders of Iowa. Cousin Ella was tall, skinny, prim. If not an actual old maid, she was one in character. Severe, critical, she was no person for a child to go for. Squeezed in between her and Father, I was aware that my presence gave her no pleasure.

Our ride started out propitiously[25] enough. It was a clear Sunday morning. Consequently, I was dressed in my Sunday best; shiny patent leather slippers, and a big flowery leghorn hat[26] with streamers down the back that I loved. Cousin Ella was nicely dressed. She wore a dark dress, a small hat, and a string of pearls. I wouldn't doubt that Dad, a classy dresser then, wore a top hat.

Dirt roads between towns were fairly well-traveled. Side roads were little more that ruts through tall grass, worn by wagon wheels and trudging hooves. Unfortunately, Dad took us down one of those rutted side roads. As I recall, he was showing Cousin Ella land that he owned. We were traveling along nicely until we struck a place where water from a recent rain had inundated the road so Dad couldn't see where it went. So he went where the road wasn't, which was off the end of a culvert, overturning the buggy, and dumping us all in the water.

Naturally, Dad's first reaction was to hold the horses lest they run away. How he got the buggy upright and back on the road I don't know. My concern was all for my beautiful and beloved hat, which was fast floating away from me. Somehow that was retrieved and Dad helped me out of the water.

Cousin Ella was frantically fishing for her string of pearls that had been torn from her neck. Dad couldn't leave the horses to help her hunt as there was nothing to tie them to. So, he promised her he'd come back the next day with help, when the water would have hopefully abated, and look for the pearls. (Which he did. They were found.)

We must have been some mess, all soggy wet, soaked to the skin, as we drove back to town. And I imagine that Dad's hope of converting Ella to a love of Iowa's land evaporated much more quickly than the water from our drenched apparel!

Perhaps Dad didn't consider Mother competent to drive his spirited horses, especially when her passengers were children. When she went driving, she drove the baggage horse, so called because he was one of a team that pulled the dray that took drummer's trunks from the depot to hotel sample rooms. With this horse, she'd pile a bunch of us kids and our friends in her surrey, and drive out into the woods for a picnic, to a slow-flowing creek (we called it a crik) where we could go wading, or just to pick wild flowers.

Iowa's untamed, unfenced prairie was a riot of wildflowers growing in tall grasses. Tiger-lilies, sweet William, black-eyed Susans, almost any wildflower you could ask for! And cattails! Mother loved cattails, and always had them in some sort of decoration in her rooms. So we kids would wade into the swamps and get them for her.

One day things didn't go so smoothly. My habit for teasing, and otherwise getting into mischief, sometimes tried my mother's patience to the limit. This day it led to near disaster. In retaliation for my teasing, one of my friends grabbed my cap and tossed it out of the buggy. "Stop, stop!" I yelled to Mother. "I've lost my cap."

By the time the buggy had stopped, my cap was some ways behind us. Evidently the horse wanted to know what was taking so long to get it, for he turned his head back to investigate. In doing so, he caught one line under the shaft. He was a slow and easy horse, but accustomed to backing drays around, so when Mother, not noticing the line was caught, pulled on it, the horse started backing and backed us into the ditch, upsetting the buggy, tumbling us out into the tall grass.

Fortunately none of us were hurt, but when Mother tried to drive the horse to pull the buggy out of the ditch, she discovered that the shaft was broken. As far as we could see, there was no house for miles. And as you may have guessed, no convenient phone booth along the road from which we could call for help.

Happily, those horses were so hard worked that when they got a chance to stand still, they did; as did this one while Mother stepped out into the middle of the road and in a loud voice yelled, "Help, help!" One of our regular boarders, who had a farm several miles from where we were, jokingly told Mother after he'd heard her story, "So you were the one making all that racket! I heard several cries, but couldn't figure out who in the devil it could be, so I let it pass!"

It was nearing late afternoon, we were much too far from town to walk, and Mother was getting nervous, when about a half a mile down the road she saw a wisp of smoke spiraling up out of a grove. A grove in that area indicated that a house might be there, so she sent two of us down the road to see if we could dig up help. We found a man and his son, in a shed, working on a piece of machinery. The smoke we had seen was from his forge. When we recounted our catastrophe, he gathered up what tools he felt he might need, and he and his son came to our rescue.

The surrey was soon out of the ditch, the shaft temporarily fixed, and sound enough to get us back to town. We managed to get home without further mishap, but, naturally, forever after, that accident was blamed on me!

Buggy riding was one of our favorite pastimes, and the young man who had a horse and smart rig was the regular guy, just as later in the early days of cars, the boy who had the use of his parent's automobile, was the fellow the girls went for.

Though almost everyone in town "who was somebody" had a horse and buggy, and a barn back of the house, the smartest rig in town belonged to "Aunt Minnie" Willson, daughter-in-law of our town's founder. She drove a team of spirited Palominos, and her surrey, "with the fringe on top", was almost the exact color of her steeds. She herself was a natural blonde, her hair piled high on her head, much the same color as her team and rig. Plump, an asset in those days, with large hips and bust, and laced-in waist, she dressed beautifully, so all eyes were turned in her direction as she drove down the street. When Mother and I were her passengers, I felt very important.

Formal calling was the thing in those days. When Mother went to call she hired a broughman and team from the livery stable, using our hotel porter as driver. Sometimes she'd take me and my two year old brother, Maris, with her. Maris, dressed in a Little Lord Fauntleroy suit (a role that suited him not at all!) would sit up front with the driver. I, dressed as a little lady (a role that suited me neither, but which I loved to play!) would sit beside Mother. As Maris could never be depended upon to behave, he was never allowed to go into the house with Mother. While I, on the other hand, loved to go with her, and knowing we would be served cakes and tea, always did behave. If the maid who answered the door announced that her mistress was not in, Mother would drop her card on a small silver tray on the hall table. <u>Everybody</u> had a maid in those days. Why not? The price of one was three dollars a week.

With horses a necessity, the blacksmith shop in our town never hurt for trade. The shop was next to my father's hotel, and sometime when I'd run out of interesting things to do, I'd go there and watch the smithy shoe the horses. Protected by a flapping leather apron split almost to the  waist, standing with his back to the horse, he would pick up the horse's foot, hold it firmly between his knees, and nail on a shoe. His trimming of the hoof always made me wince a little. "Doesn't it hurt him?" I'd ask. "Does it hurt when you trim your toe nails?" The smithy would reply to my plaint. "This is the same thing."

Generally a horse would stand quietly, head lowered, and some accustomed to this treatment, would almost go to sleep. Again a horse might rip and snort, rearing up on his hind legs, he'd paw the air. I'd back away, fearful that he'd break loose, and in his rush for escape, run over me. Somehow the smithy brought even the most cantankerous under control. I liked the smithy. Careful that I didn't get hurt, he'd joke with me, as a child likes to be joked with.

I'd follow him to the back of the shop where he pumped the bellows of the forge until the coals turned a fiery red, and a flurry of golden sparks flew up into the air. Fascinated, I'd watch while the horse shoe he laid on the coals heated until it glowed, after which  he'd lay it on the anvil and pound it into whatever shape he wanted. That done, holding it with a forceps, he'd plunge it into a pail of cold water that steamed and sizzled as the hot iron struck it. When it was cool, he'd carry it back to nail on to the waiting hoof.

The shop was off limits to my small brother Maris, but sometimes he'd escape by the hotel kitchen door and wander into the wide back door of the shop. He was as fascinated as I was by that fiery shoe lying on the anvil, and one day, when the smithy's back was turned, he picked it up. His screams alerted everyone to action. Someone rushed him to my mother. The doctor was called, and came running. It was a long time before that ugly wound healed.

Another of my hangouts, when things were dull, was the livery stable across the street. Here, I'd go visit Mr. Lasher. He and his wife were good friends of my parents, and I always felt welcome there. I might hope he was going someplace where he could take me with him for the ride. Or he might walk me down the "aisle", the soft carpet of straw between the rows of twenty or so horses, who, with their noses in their feed boxes, would turn to look at us as we passed. I'd ask Mr. Lasher questions about them. Who did this horse belong to? What were their names? Which were my father's?

Most of the horses, with a vehicle, were for hire; others were boarders whose owners had no barn or didn't want the care of them. In the front of the stable were vehicles, tongues or shafts standing straight up.

Runabouts, spring wagons, surreys, or common one-seated buggies with tops that could be put up or down.

The barn I liked best was "Aunt Minnie's."[27] It was back of her house, only a little way down the alley from the hotel back yard, so I could get there easy. As she had a small son, Walter, it was a gathering place for the neighborhood kids. It also had several kinds of vehicles we could play in, pretending we were driving, really going places.

And how we'd play! We'd whip our "horses," struggle with them when they didn't behave; say whoa, geddap, gee, haw. Pretend! Taking just what we had and making our own world of it.

Better yet, we liked to play in the haymow, climb up the ladder, crawl through the small opening at the top, and romp in the hay, rolling, sliding down! Sometimes we'd hang from the broad heavy beams, or the most courageous of us would walk them, confident that if we fell there'd be a soft cushion of hay to land in. Only after a small friend of mine fell through the hole down which they pushed the hay to the horses, and broke her arm, was the haymow taboo to me.

But I wasn't the sort of child to stay below, listening to the fun and laughter going on above me. So I was easy bait to the coaxing, "Oh, come on, Irene. Your mother won't find out!" Of course not! How could she?

But mothers have ways! Mine did. One night as she was unbuttoning my dress, getting me ready for bed, she said sharply, "Young lady, you've been playing up in Willson's haymow again!"

Amazed, giving myself away, I gasped out, "How did you know?" "This way!" She turned around to show me a long strand of hay. "This was inside your dress." Woe to me! I was always the sort of child who could never do anything wrong without being found out.

A HISTORY LESSON!

Sometimes when there were no other kids around to play with, I'd skip across the alley to Aunt Minnie's.[27] Not to see her, but to visit with Grandma Willson. She and her husband, Walter, lived with Frank, their only child, and his wife, Minnie. Grandpa Willson, as I called him, was a short man, bald on top of his head, he had a heavy grey beard that stuck out from his chin like a billy goat's whiskers. Sprucely dressed, when not busy at some of his many activities, he was an energetic old man who took active interest in the business of the town he had founded.

Grandma Willson was a dainty little lady who always wore delicate black silk dresses, high of neck, with long sleeves, just the shiny tips of her shoes showing beneath the hem of her long skirts. She was lame, and I often amused myself by walking with her crutches. Since I was large for my age and she small, they almost fit me. I used to wish that someday when I grew up something would happen to me so that I would have to use crutches.

I liked best to sit on a low stool near her as she sat in her rocker, knitting, or tatting, and listen to her tell of pioneer days and their arrival in the town that was then called Newcastle. She made those times come alive for me, and I was forever begging for more stories. She told me how they, and Grandpa's brother, Summer, left their home in Wisconsin in October of 1854 and went by rail to Rockford Illinois, which was as far as the railroad went at that time.

There they bought horses and equipment for their long trek across the prairie to Newcastle, Iowa, which Grandpa Willson had previously investigated and decided that was where he wanted to settle. They had expected to stay in Rockford until the Mississippi froze over and they could cross on the ice; there was no bridge over the river then and the ferry ran only in the summer months.

During that very night, a cake of ice about a mile long floated downstream and lodged between the two shores and they decided to cross on that. It was a perilous journey. I was frightened just to hear her tell of the danger as the water swirled around and even over the ice as they crossed. Fortunately, the trip went without mishap.

The crossing of the prairie was also dangerous. Grandpa Willson said that "No one can imagine the hardships we endured." Coming to one creek that had no bridge, and was too deep for the horses to ford, they had to camp there until the men built a bridge, standing waist deep in icy water to do so.

When they finally arrived at Newcastle, they stayed with other settlers while Grandpa and Summer built a log cabin. Supplies were short and they were able to buy only one door for the two doors planned, so they had to hang a quilt in the second doorway.

Once in their own home, not a person came to their door who wasn't welcomed, given food, and if possible, bedded down. The words of welcome then were "the latch string is always out", and theirs certainly was. The Willson cabin very quickly became a kind of hotel for new settlers and land prospectors. Not a day after they were settled in, reported Grandma Willson, but she fed from forty to one hundred persons at every meal! The food left much to be desired: hominy, cornbread, salt pork, possibly turnips, coffee, and if the men were lucky in their hunting, they might have wild game.

After his own house was finished, Grandpa Willson built more log cabins. Then, he acquired a sawmill, from which the first boards went into the home of Bradford Mason. He had the first frame house in town. Bradford's son, Bridgeman, (who eventually became my father-in-law) was the first white child born in the settlement.[28]

As so many settlers and land seekers were constantly arriving, Grandpa Willson soon realized that a real hotel was needed. He and Summer built a frame hotel in the southeastern end of town, at the corner of Bank and Seneca streets, and named it the Webster City Hotel. The name of Newcastle for the town had been discarded in favor of Webster City. As the hotel faced the city park, it later became known as the Park Hotel.

Much of the land both in and surrounding Webster City was swamp land, or sloughs, as they were then called. A man trekking across country, when he came to a slough, would remove his boots and socks, roll up his trousers, and wade across it, donning his clothes on the farther side. If his destination were any distance away, he might have to put on several repeat performances. Women, too, Grandma Willson testified, going to visit a neighbor, might have to go through the same ritual, lifting their skirts only as high as modesty allowed.

Talk of a railroad soon to come through town caused great excitement, and there was much discussion as to where the depot should be located. The majority of people wanted it located at the north end of Seneca street, then the main "drag" of the town, but the Willson's, who with a few of their friends owned most of the land in the western part of town, wanted the depot there.

"The railroad decided the issue," Grandma Willson said. "They did not want it at the end of Seneca street as that was too near the river, so a small brick depot was built where we had wanted it." Though they had nothing to do with the railroad decision, the blame for the location was put on them. So much controversy and hard feelings arose because of this that Grandpa Willson pulled up stakes and built a wooden frame hotel a few blocks west of Seneca street.

Everyone laughed and ridiculed his move because this part of town was mainly swamp land. In fact, between the hotel and the proposed depot site was a large swamp several blocks long. Called the Black Swamp, it was where the men in town went duck hunting. Everyone said that, "Walt Willson will see the folly of his decision and come back to the old stand, on dry ground, a poorer but wiser man."

"But they didn't know the man with whom they were dealing," laughed Grandma Willson. "Walt was a man of great pluck, vigor, and foresight, and once he made a decision, he never turned back." As soon as his hotel was completed, he built a row of stores along Main or Second street, offering a year's free rent to any who set up business in them, with low rents for several years after. He also offered a free building lot to anyone who purchased a lot to be used for a home!

This offer was so good that business was soon thriving. This new section became the main business part of town, known as Willson Town, and those who had so freely ridiculed Grandpa Willson's wild schemes were soon eating their words.

When bricks became available around 1885, the Willson's tore down their frame hotel and erected a three story brick hotel (four stories with the basement) on the same site. Grandma Willson would smile and end our visit with the words, "This was the hotel your father later bought, Irene, and that's how you happen to be living in Webster City, Iowa."

OUR TOWN

Grandma Willson's accounts of the history of Webster City renewed my interest in the town in which I lived. Returning home after a visit with her, I would become keenly aware of my surroundings, and I would keep my eyes open trying to visualize the town as she described it. This exercise was good for me; I developed an awareness of the growth and change that had taken place in the town in previous years, and my perception of Webster City increased.

My first memories are of riding my tricycle back and forth on the wide front porch of our hotel, and it is from that vantage point that I got my first impressions of the town. On the other three corners with the hotel stood substantial brick buildings.

Directly across from the hotel was the Hamilton County bank; on the third story of the building the Elks Lodge held forth, and most of the town's social activities took place. "Kitty-corner" from the hotel was the Webster City Savings Bank; on the upper story of this bank was the Willson

61

Opera house, a somewhat palatial place for so small a town, where the townsfolk came for entertainment.

In the third building was a drug store, one of my favorite spots as I grew older. Here I'd sit at the counter devouring ice cream sodas (sundaes were still a treat of the future) and gabbing with "Dad" Neuman, the druggist and a friend of every kid in town.

In the rear of the store were several shelves of doll heads for which I was a steady customer. Bisque or china, curly-headed blondes or brunettes. Whenever I broke one of my own doll heads I'd skip across the street, pick out a new head, and scamper back to have my mother sew it onto the leather body of my recently decapitated doll.

Here, too, Junie and I sold whiskey bottles for one, two, or three cents each. We made regular tours through the hotel, opening bureau drawers, looking for "dead soldiers" that imbibing traveling men had emptied and left behind. We never grew rich at this business, but often got enough to gloat over!

On each side of the hotel ran wide dirt streets, Main or Second, and Des Moines

62

streets. Main street was flanked by store buildings of one or two stories, fronted by board walks along which ran rows of hitching posts for the convenience of farmers who drove their buggies or wagons to town to trade.

The little brick Illinois Central depot at the north end of Des Moines street I knew well, for from there I went often to visit my grandparents in Ft. Dodge, twenty miles away.

Toward the southern end of Main Street our court house, a pretentious brick building with a jail in the basement, was said to be the best in the County. Surrounded by a beautiful lawn, it was flanked by an attractive well-shaded Court House Park.

There was a band stand in the middle of the park, and, once a week during the warm weather months, a band concert attracted almost everyone in town who was able to walk. Here we kids could romp in and out among the crowd almost free of parental control. A delicious aroma emanated from the horse-drawn popcorn stand,

keeping the vendor busy doling out bags of popcorn for five cents a bag. The other half of the block was the fenced in school yard –

boys on one side, girls on the other. Here stood the old high school, ancient even when I knew it, and the new elementary school which I attended.

Webster City was a church going town. The town had eight churches, all within a few blocks of each other, and people really went to church! With no country club, no golf course, no cars to take them places, if they  wanted to meet people, or "Belong" to something, church was about the only place the townspeople could go on Sunday.

Though swamps still existed in parts of outlying farmlands, they became non-existent around town. The reason: In 1883, three men, Charlie Soule, Jacob Maris Funk, and a Mr. Hages, built a tile factory in an outlying district in the western end of town. When placed in ditches, drainage tiles were successful in draining excess water from an area. Hence, land which was once considered useless swamp became valuable farm land.

This proved to be a welcome benefit to Webster City, and the local paper, the Freeman, offered its praise, "This is the beginning of what promises to be an important addition to the business industries of

Webster City, and is in the hands of men who have the capital and the energy to make a success of it." It was later reported, "In all the history of our country up to this time, no business enterprise has contributed more than this one to the material advancement of our people. Its smoking kilns have burned the tiles that have transformed hundreds of worthless tracts of land into the richest of agricultural fields."

The Charlie Soule's were good friends of my parents and Jacob Funk[29] played a small part in my brother's life. He was a boarder at the hotel for as long as I can remember. A short, stocky Dutchman, he had come west and bought up a lot of Iowa's land. He also had stock in the tile factory and in our hotel. Unmarried and quite wealthy, he had, so far as could be seen, no interest in women whatsoever. Friendly, quiet, unobtrusive, well-liked by our help, he was apparently a loner. Though doubtless he had activities of which I, a child, knew nothing, I remember him best sitting in a rocker in our hotel office.

Like many others, he admired my mother. When she was about to have her third child, Mr. Funk told her that if she would name the baby after him, (provided it was a boy) he'd give him forty acres of land. Now forty acres of Iowa's land was not to be sneezed at, and Mother laughingly agreed. The baby was a boy, and my parents named him Jacob Maris Merrill,[30] and, true to his promise, Mr. Funk gave my brother his forty acres of land!

Another one of our boarders, Mr. Banks, was an important citizen of Webster City, and served as our mayor for many years. A thin, wiry, frail-looking little man, he possessed unusual energy and was still the mayor of our town when, at the age of 92, he died.

Prior to his death, he had been ill for quite some time. In fact, he had "hung so long at death's door," that because of his prominence, the local paper had a long obituary written up in advance to publish the moment he died.

The trouble was, they printed his obituary before he died! Somehow the rumor got out that his end had come, and without verifying the story, the paper ran the obituary. Mr. Banks lived several days after its printing; this may be the only instance where a man was privileged to read his own obituary!

Our town had its share of inventors, and I think it is worthy to note that the first typewriter was invented in Webster City. The inventor was Samuel Boxter. But, the typewriter lay in his home for forty years, forgotten even by him. In the late 1860's, another Webster City man, Abner Peeler, a jeweler, perfected an invention for writing with type which so attracted the attention of his employer, William Crosley, that he took Peeler and the machine to Washington to take out a patent.

The attorney who wrote the papers necessary to receive the patent, did not, in his document, make the description cover the principle discovered in this respect. So the patent proved to be defective, and was later taken up by strangers who had no right to it. Like many men of great genius, Peeler had little business ability, and after losing interest in his typewriter, he invented an engraving machine, a knitting machine, and still later perfected an improvement for the Singer sewing machine.

I'm sure it would be foolish for me to say that the first automobile was also invented in our town. I'd soon have criticism flying at me from all sides! But, one day, shortly after the turn of the century, people were amazed to see an ordinary one-seated buggy, minus shafts and horse, rolling down our street. Two men were riding in it, the one on the <u>right</u> holding a stick with which he apparently guided this odd contraption. Whatever propelled it was entirely invisible.

This "horseless carriage," was the first auto I'd ever seen. The men riding in it, brothers who owned a bicycle shop, were its inventors. People's amazement turned slowly to amusement, from amusement to ridicule. If anyone thought that such a contraption would ever put the horse out of business, <u>well,</u> perhaps they'd better have their heads examined!

FIRE!

A fire was a big event in the small town where I grew up, and if physically possible, I never missed going to one. After all, when an occasional street fair, carnival, circus, or show were our only exciting events, a fire was too big an entertainment to miss.

Our fire whistle made a sound that could wake the dead. Let me hear it, even in the middle of the night, and I was up, pulling on my clothes, to hot foot it to the scene of the action. The turmoil, the lights, the unwinding of the hose from the horse-drawn wagon; the firemen shouting orders to one another, the flames sending sparks toward the sky, the jostling of the crowd – what child could remain in bed when all that was going on?

The biggest, most exciting fire I ever went to – big because it was a department store occupying two buildings – brought out most of the town. It had a good start before being discovered, so the whole building was in flames by the time I arrived. Though I stood jammed in among the crowd on the other side of the street, the flames were so hot they almost scorched my cheeks.

Since the building was a goner, the main efforts of the firemen, water gushing from their hoses, were to save the adjoining buildings, for once they caught, the whole of our main street might have gone up in flames. It was well into daylight before the fire was conquered enough so that the crowd dispersed to go home and eke out what sleep they could. As a safeguard, water was played over the smoldering ruins most of the next day.

But one fire I'll not forget was one I didn't travel far to see. My friend Junie was staying the night with me, as we had plans for early morning. When the whistle sounded, I listened to the "toots" which could tell us in which ward the fire was raging. "Junie," I cried as we clambered into our clothes, "That's this ward. The fire must be near here – maybe in one of the stores."

How right I was! My bedroom window overlooked the hotel backyard and suddenly, conscious of  commotion out there, I glanced out just in time to see the fire engine hove into view and smoke pouring from the furnace door. Even as I was digesting this fact, George, our yardman, knocked on my door to tell me I'd better get out as the hotel was on fire.

Instantly Junie and I went into action. The one thing I knew must be saved from the fire was an heirloom chest, which in my childish dreams I envisioned becoming my hope chest, to be filled to the brim with fine linens, laces, and the other beautiful articles given to young ladies in love at bridal showers. The chest had been made out of an intricately hand-carved bed that I'd been born in. It was about four feet long and certainly not an easy article to carry down the fire escape! Nevertheless, the chest had to be saved, so I inveigled George to do just that. How he ever got it out the window and down the ladder I still don't understand, but he did and Junie and I climbed down the ladder after him. Which was as ridiculous a means of escape as one can imagine.

For right across the hall from my bedroom door was the back stairs leading into the kitchen. It would have been so simple to have carried that box out that way, through the dining room, office, onto the porch. But smoke was already seeping through the halls and we expected flames momentarily to engulf us.

Actually the fire – spontaneous combustion in the coal pit – was quickly conquered, and only one ell of the hotel burned, and that not too extensively. But the whole hotel was so smoked up that much of it had to be repapered and painted.

That old, red, horse-drawn fire wagon provided us kids with another form of entertainment when things grew dull. We'd go to the firehouse and ask the firemen to hitch up the horses. Since this was a break in their monotony too, they were always glad to oblige us. They'd push a button that would ring a bell; the doors of the box stalls would fly open, the horses  would rush out, and stand on either side of the tongue of the fire wagon.

Their harness, hanging from the ceiling, would drop onto their backs. The men, sliding down the pole from the loft, would snap them into place, then climb up on the wagon, and away they'd go!

Today's fire equipment can't be beat for efficiency or life-saving, but the sight of those beautiful black horses tearing down the street, manes flying, fire bell clanging, couldn't be beat for excitement. Nor did the men mind. If fires were too far apart, they'd take the team out on practice runs to keep them in shape.

When I was much younger, another fire in the hotel, that threatened to be large, had an almost humorous ending – although I'm sure my mother didn't consider it so. Aunt Tina,[31] Mother's sister from Minneapolis, and her two small sons were visiting us. Herman, the younger, was about the age of my brother Maris. Mother and Aunt Tina were visiting in my aunt's room, across the hall from Mother's rooms, when suddenly Maris appeared at their door, wide-eyed, to exclaim, "Come quick! Big fire in there!"

You may be sure that they came quick. They found Mother's lovely lace curtains all ablaze. The boys had been playing with matches with that result. I don't remember how much damage the fire did, nor how it was extinguished. I remember only the aftermath.

Mother's two rooms had to be done over. They were already to have the furniture moved back in, when Mother was giving my brother and me a bath. As the hotel then had no regular bathroom, Mother had had made a tin tub large enough so that she could bathe two children at the same time.

On this occasion, there was not a stick of furniture in the room, with the exception of a fancy wicker table on which Mother had her favorite lamp with the beautiful round bowl with flowered shade to match. For some reason, Mother left the room for a few moments, leaving us to our own devices.

Which were far from behaving. The floor on which our tub sat had just been newly varnished. In fooling, as kids will when left alone, the soap fell out of the tub and I got out to get it, thereby discovering that the newly varnished floor was slick as glass. So I started sliding over it on my bare bottom. And my brother, seeing what fun I was having, joined me. We'd give ourselves a push that sent us across the room, then back again.

How often we did this before catastrophe occurred I've no idea. But unexpectedly one of us bumped into the wicker table, Mother's lamp fell over and shattered on the floor. Mother, wherever she was, heard the crash and came running. If our bottoms weren't already red from our sliding, they were when SHE got through with us!

OUT OF LINE!

One law about which our father was adamant was never, <u>never</u> should we ask a traveling man for money. If one proffered a penny or a nickel, as they frequently did, we could accept it. But if we asked, dire were the consequences.

Joe was not a transient. He worked for us and he owed me a nickel. So one day when my friend Junie and I had a yen for candy, I decided to ask Joe to pay up.

Junie and I, life-long friends, were as inseparable as Siamese twins. We did everything together. She ate and slept at my house, I slept and ate at hers. If I took music lessons, she took music lessons. If she took dancing lessons, I did too. We even had matching dresses. She was a year older than I, but I always insisted that someday I'd catch up with her. As we grew older, I was willing to leave things as they were.

Joe gave me the nickel. But with that nickel clutched in my hand I decided that one nickel between two candy-hungry kids wasn't enough. Better if we each had a nickel, so I said, "I'll hide this nickel and ask my father for one."

I was wearing a sailor cap with a tight band, and I stuck the nickel up under it. Feeling it was safe from discovery, I went to see my father. He was sick in bed. Standing beside his bed, with Junie close to me, I made my request.

My father looked at me a long moment before he asked, "Where did you get that nickel you have?" "What nickel?" (I guess my voice squeaked a little as I asked that!) "The one that's sliding down from under your cap," Dad replied calmly.

Horrified, I slapped my hand up against my head. Sure enough! That nickel had slipped halfway from under its hiding place. "Joe—Joe gave it to me," I confessed. So came the inevitable question, "Did you ask him for it?" "Y-yes," I stammered, adding as quickly as my tongue could manage it, "But he owed it to me."

No difference! I'd broken an inviolate rule. Sick though he was, he could move quickly. Before I knew it, he sat up and pulled me over his knee and let me have it. Not only did I not get a second nickel, but sobbing all the way back downstairs, I had to return the one I had.

Another fiasco with my father concerned money. Each time I passed a grade in school he gave me a dollar. But that gave me no thrill. I couldn't spend it. It had to go in my bank.

One day, however, I went a bit wild. I was with a small friend whose father owned a drug store. On our way home from school we stopped there. The first thing I noticed was a big bowl of rubber balls, all sizes, and colors! My weakness was rubber balls; I love them. I picked up a beautiful multi-colored one. Just the size to play jacks with.

For some inexplicable reason I had my dollar with me, not yet banked, burning a hole in my pocket. So I bought that ball, and some jacks to go with it. Once broken, that dollar might as well be spent. I bought a tablet and a pencil with a fancy top, a pencil box, chalk and eraser, just like we used in school, for my blackboard, some crayolas, and a coloring book. I spent the money I had left over at the candy store.

I didn't expect my father to discover these weighty transactions. How he learned, I'll never know. He made me return every item I'd bought at the drug store and put the money in my bank. The candy I couldn't return as my friend and I had eaten it.

Once a traveling man gave me a dollar. A <u>whole</u> dollar! A man I'd never even seen before. "Go buy yourself some candy," he said.

"A whole dollar for <u>candy</u>?" I looked at him in utter disbelief. That's what he meant. What's more, he walked with me to that same penny candy store to help me make my selections. How often had I stopped on my way to school with just one penny to spend, drooling before that glass case, suffering as I tried to decide what I wanted. Now I had enough money to buy everything my heart desired.

My new friend stood beside me as I pointed. Some of that, one of these, a box of those, chocolate creams, pink marshmallow bananas, long red sticks of licorice, "fried eggs" in cunning little dishes. Never was a child so near heaven.

I left that store with a bag of candy as big as the bags they fill at super markets. What's more, my good traveling man carried it home for me. About this my father could do nothing. By the time he learned of it, the man was gone. I never saw him again. But he'll always remain one of my childhood idols.

One of Dad's friends, a rich architect, was a heavy-set, jolly, well-dressed man for whom I'll always have a soft spot in my heart. He came to the hotel a lot, and whenever he'd see me he'd say, "Hello Sweetheart. How's my Sweetheart today?" Then he'd put his hand in his pocket and pull out a dime. No wonder I loved him; a dime was a small fortune to me.

I never seemed able to keep out of trouble. Often, on pleasant summer evenings, after the children were in bed, asleep, Mother would go down and sit on the porch and visit with my father. As I was the oldest, it didn't matter whether or not I was asleep. I was left sort of in charge of the situation.

But Mother had a fear about someone sneaking up the backstairs and invading our room, to steal us or do harm, and the fear infected me. Every noise I'd hear, including the sound of someone coming up the stairs which might only be one of the help, would frighten me. So one night I finally found a solution to the difficulty. I awakened the baby, who naturally started to cry, then rang the bell for the porter. When he arrived I asked him to tell Mama that the baby was awake and crying.

Mother came upstairs. By the time she had the baby quieted and back to sleep, it was too late to rejoin Dad. So she stayed and went to bed, which was exactly what I wanted her to do.

This had worked so perfectly, that, discarding discretion, I tried a repeat performance the next night. This time things didn't work out so well. It was so unusual for the baby to awaken, once asleep, that Mother's suspicions were aroused. When she confronted me, (one of my few virtues was that I wasn't a good liar!) the guilt in my face gave me away.

Mother's spankings were customarily with the back of a hair brush. This night she was so angry she gave no heed to which side she used, and by chance it was the bristle side. Which wouldn't have been so bad except that the brush was a wire hair brush, commonly used because the wire bristles got the snarls out of a child's hair more easily. But used as Mother used it, it also peppered my bottom with tiny red polka dots.

Blood! Was Mother then ever contrite! She bathed and salved my injured anatomy, hugged, and tucked me, still crying, into bed. She didn't go back down with Dad that night either. Nor did I ever try that trick again!

Unfortunately, my affinity for trouble did not cease when I was with friends. Hence, Junie and I, when together, frequently found ourselves in Dutch. We loved to dress up in Mother's clothes and play lady. With certain dresses, Mother allowed this. But as we sometimes used our own discretion, one day as she was going out, her parting words were, "Now don't you children get into any of my <u>good</u> clothes."

We were tired of the dresses we were allowed to use. When we went to her closet to get them, and saw so many lovely dresses hanging there, the temptation was great, and we fell. Silks, satins, velvets! We chose dresses with long trains. We each donned one of Mother's small fancy hats, and rummaged in her bureau for long gloves. And fans! A necessity for any lady back then.

We were standing in her bedroom window, which overlooked the backyard, hands in long gloves, using our fans discreetly, chatting merrily away as we felt ladies would. A sudden, "Hello there!" interrupted our conversation and directed our attention to outside where we saw Mother just coming in to the backyard.

Mother said afterwards that she had never seen two heads disappear more quickly. We just vanished. She thought nothing of it for when she came up to her rooms, we were playing quietly, behaving as good children should. Not until later when she found all her good dresses, hats, gloves, and fans heaped in a pile of the closet floor did she understand the disappearance of those two small heads from the window. As soon as Mother appeared, Junie, with good reason, disappeared entirely and so I, alone, was the one who got the "dressing down."

My grandfather was a trader. He generally came out ahead and how he'd chuckle when he did! Maybe I inherited my expert trading ability from him. My tender was oranges I'd take from the hotel kitchen. I'd trade them with my schoolmates for anything that they had that I wanted. Eight, ten, twelve, oranges – however many it took to get what I desired. Once I traded a dozen oranges for a batch of paper dolls a girl had cut out of magazines.

But my biggest trade was for a stamp collection. One of my schoolmates had an uncle in the army. His letters carried stamps from all over the world. The boy brought this collection to show our class at school. How I wanted those stamps! I had to work hard to make that trade. I began low, and offered eight oranges, then ten – and worked up until the boy was satisfied with twenty-two.

Naturally I couldn't bring all those oranges to school at once. Girls wore full blouses then, and I'd take two or three from the bowl in the dining room, hide them in the front of my blouse, then watch for a chance to sneak out of the room and past the desk clerk without being seen. It took a long time to get those twenty-two oranges paid off. That was probably the first instance of paying on the installment plan!

Another orange deal of mine didn't turn out so well. At school a girl gave me an orange which turned out to be, when peeled, a blood orange. Never having seen such an oddity, I asked the girl where she had gotten it. She wasn't sure. Some had been found in a dozen oranges her father had bought. She warned me that you couldn't count on them. Sometimes there'd only be three or four in a dozen.

If three or four blood oranges might be found in a dozen, I reasoned as I skipped home from school that day, how many might be found in a whole crate? As my father bought oranges for the hotel by the crate, it was up to me to go a-seeking.

Fruit was kept in the first compartment of the hotel refrigerator. It was customary for me, without a "hello" or "may I?," to scavenge around in there after school for something to eat. So the chef, or whoever might find me there, would think nothing of it.

This day they should have been on their guard. For I was on a hunt for a blood orange. As the skin of the orange I'd eaten wasn't red, giving no indication of the red inside, the inside was where I'd have to look. The way I intended to go about it was to poke a hole in every orange until I found a bloody one. Crouched down beside the crate of oranges, I went about it methodically.

When I heard anyone approaching, I'd jump up quickly and pretend to be looking for something to eat, so usual a thing that anyone entering thought nothing of it. As the room was lighted only by a dim light bulb, no one noticed what was being done to the crate of oranges.

It took quite a while to go through the whole crate. It's odd no one got suspicious. What I got from that experience was, not a single blood orange in the whole lot. What I did get, however, was a good whipping. It seems that when the damaged oranges were discovered, everybody remembered seeing me in the refrigerator. So, at least a certain part of my anatomy turned red!

How the chef contrived to use those damaged oranges, I don't know. Maybe in orange float pudding. Or orange upside down cake. It's for certain that they weren't used in orange juice. A glass of orange juice at breakfast then was not essential. No one knew anything about Vitamin C – or about any of its sisters and brothers. Oranges were for eating, not drinking. And certainly those oranges I'd damaged could not be served as they were, in the dining room.

Another incident that turned out better had to do with the fruit that was Eve's downfall. I was visiting my grandparents in their private home in Minneapolis, where three barrels of apples were stored in their cellar. Every fall Grandfather, having been born in Vermont, sent back home for his favorite apples. The moment the cellar door was opened, the fragrance of those barrels of fruit floated up like a perfume.

One day I was going shopping with my grandparents. Grandmother told me I could get an apple to eat on the way downtown. Since we were going in horse and buggy, the trip would take some time.

I crept down the stairs into the dark cellar, chose an apple from a barrel, then thinking two might be better, (my habitual reasoning that "two might be better than one" was often my downfall!) I took a second apple and tucked it away in my blouse.

I remember my grandmother so well that day. She was wearing a long black cape with a small hat on her grey hair, the inevitable ribbons tied under her chin. We were walking along the street very sedately when that apple dropped out of my blouse and rolled down the walk ahead of us. I held my breath as Grandmother, looking at that rolling fruit, said in astonishment; "Well where did that come from?"

As if to find out, she turned around. We had just passed a fruit stand where a man, of all things, stood polishing apples. "Well, what do you know about that!" Grandmother said indignantly. "That man must have thrown that fruit after you."

I said not a word. My breath of relief was long and heartfelt. Grandmother, still perturbed by such insolence, turned back and we continued on down the street with dignity.

THAT'S ENTERTAINMENT

Perhaps those who live in today's fabulous world of radio, TV, movies, wonder what kids of our era did for amusement. The questioner might be surprised at the many opportunities we had for fun. Much that we did had to depend on do-it-yourself stuff. But that very thing was good for our initiative, ingenuity, and creativeness. While today's way of being entertained is apt to dampen, if not actually damage those traits.

Instead of getting in a car and seeking pleasures far afield, much of our fun centered around our homes. Get a bunch of kids together and they were sure to find ways to have fun. Doubtless this depended upon the patience of many a mother who might have wished for a movie to which she might send her over-active child so that she could have a little peace, instead of listening to the plaint, "Mother, what can I do? The kids want a taffy pull. Can we have one here?"

So a mother would sometimes relent and let a child invite in friends – and how we all loved that! Standing by, noisily talking and laughing, while the mother boiled the delicious smelling molasses concoction to the right consistency! Waiting for it to cool, and then grabbing up a handful of the gooey mixture to pull.

Two pulling together was the most fun. We'd string it out to its safest length, slipping it together and pulling it out again. But what a toll it took on mothers! What a mess! A dozen boys and girls, hands gooey, leaving a smear of taffy on everything they touched.

Two schools of thought on taffy pulling existed. One claimed that taffy stuck less by wetting one's hands, the other believed smearing the hands with butter was the better method. Finally, the sticky substance developed to a consistency that could be pulled out to a thin twisted strip and snipped into small pieces with scissors. But for pure fun, the pulling beat the eating!

Popcorn-ball parties were equally fun. Here, too, mother had to watch the boiling of the molasses, but we kids had the fun of popping the corn on the big coal range. We popped it either in a big covered iron skillet with plenty of lard or in a wire basket with a long handle, keeping the corn always moving so it wouldn't burn. When there was a full dishpan of the snowy corn, the patient hostess would pour the sticky molasses over it, we'd grab up handfuls of the stuff and mold it into balls. Here, too, the fun was in the making rather than the eating, for when the eating was done, everyone went home.

Birthday parties! A bunch of noisy boys and girls, too often rough and tumbly, a mother and probably a helper, trying to tone them down, get them playing games. Hide the thimble, button-button who's got the button, musical chairs, boys pushing the girls away so they wouldn't be the ones losing out. Post-office was a favorite—for the kids who were popular. But too often it was the same boys and girls called into a dark hall or closet for a postage stamp. A slobbery kiss, a peck on the cheek, a girl coming out, cheeks blushing. Then there was that shy little wall-flower waiting so hopefully to hear her name called and when it was, by a boy she detested.

It was at parties that we had our most fun, and telling ghost stories was what we loved best. Getting all shivery as we listened to tales of squeaking doors, clanking chains, hollow footsteps shuffling down a haunted hall! Unless, unbeknownst to me, today's boys and girls are keeping such games alive, they're as dead as the ghosts we shivered over.

Raking leaves may not sound like fun, but what a ball we made of it! I so well remember those soft fall evenings, big heaps of leaves burning along the edges of our dirt streets. Their pungent smoke filled the air with that special fragrance that comes only at this time of year. Their bright flames pushing back the growing darkness, sending bright sparks up into the air, or smoldering down until a fresh armful of leaves brought them back to life.

Let us see some friend's father out raking leaves and we'd rush over to help. How much help we might be was questionable, but whoever it was seemed glad enough to have us to hunt up whatever extra rakes he might have. Those who had no rakes would gather up armloads of leaves, pack them into a big basket or wheelbarrow to be carried and dumped on the fire. Then when the work was done, our friend's mother might bring out a plate of cookies, or invite us in the house for cookies and lemonade, knowing we would be both hungry and thirsty after our labors.

"Playing out" on warm summer evenings was another way to get a gang together. "Mother, can I go over to Jennie's and play out tonight? All the kids are..." What mother hasn't been bombarded by those words, "All the kids are...Everybody's going!"

My mother, if she knew Jennie, or Jennie's mother, might say, "Yes! If you'll be home before dark."

So perhaps a dozen of the neighborhood kids would gather at Jennie's to play run sheep run, hide and seek, crack the whip—screaming and yelling when caught, or flung off the end of the cracking whip. With no cars to worry about, we had the whole road and everybody's lawn to spread out in. Finally, hot and tired, we'd plunk ourselves down on somebody's front porch to catch our breath, to rest and cool off a bit. Maybe again somebody's good mother would bring out lemonade and we'd go back to playing until darkness sent us scampering home.

Gathering around a piano and singing our favorite songs could provide a perfect evening's entertainment. Everyone who was anyone, had a piano. Every kid had suffered through the agony of music lessons, so almost everyone could play. "Down by the Old Mill Stream," "Wait Till the Sun Shines Nellie," "Under the Old Apple Tree." How we did belt out that one! Always, at the end there'd be refreshments, according to the season. Hot chocolate in winter, lemonade or ice cream in hot weather. Never ice cream in winter. It was a summer delicacy only. You couldn't buy it in winter. And though most people made their own, the old wooden freezer was put away in the fall, not to see the light of day until summer.

We varied our singing once by taking it on the run— so to speak. One warm summer evening a bunch of us hired a carryall, team and driver, and up and down Main Street entertaining the town with "Row, Row, Row Your Boat," "Tip Tip Tippy Canoe," "The Frost is on the Pumpkin." Mixing jokes, fun and laughter with our singing, we had a wonderful time. Mr. Reinecker, the driver, was liked by all who knew him, but he was a man's man.

When we went out to his farm we generally went in a buckboard pulled by a spirited team and I loved that. A buckboard, now practically extinct, was a long vehicle with several seats, which rested on a flooring of long flexible boards whose ends rested on the axles. The one we rode had a top edged with fringe and was bouncy to ride in.

The reason for having our picnic out at Mr. Reinecker's was so the men could hunt prairie chickens, with which Iowa abounded in its early years. That way the men got in a day of good sport, and everybody had good eating. The tenant lady would cook the chickens and serve us in a long dining room, it being too hot to eat in the unshaded sun outside. We kids were probably tired, cross, and sleepy after a day of playing in the haymow, sliding down the straw stack, and chasing pigs and chickens until we were caught.

The picnic which was most fun to get to was at Lehigh, a small coal-mining town far enough away that we had to go by train, the Crooked Creek Railroad,[24] which, along with the mines , was owned by Walter Willson. The train, which ran only between our town and the mines, was jiggly, slow, and dirty. The big deal was to get to ride in the cupola of the caboose from which we not only got a high view of all we passed, but were free from parental control so could fool as much as we pleased. The picnic, as usual, consisted of the men fishing, the women cooking our meal of fish, we kids playing in the river, but topping all that was our ride to and from the picnic.

Our Sunday School picnic was another event eagerly looked forward to. It was held in a park down by the river. A long white table cloth would be spread on the grass and practically covered with an array of the most delicious food one could taste. The food that made my eyes sparkle were the huge platters of deviled eggs, my favorite food. At Sunday School picnics I always got enough!

After playing in the river and getting thoroughly wet, much to the despair of our mothers, we'd have contests. Seeing who could carry an egg farthest on a spoon without dropping it, boys playing leap frog, running races, especially the one where two boys each tie one leg together in a gunny sack and hobbling along, tumbling down, getting up, hurrying to make up time till they'd reached their goal and won their prize. The day was too short. Tired but happy, we'd go home, sorry that an event to which we'd so looked forward to was over.

The ice cream social put on by the Ladies Aid Society was the big summer event in our town. Though its purpose was to raise money for the church,

it provided a delightful get-together evening for old, young, and in between. Everybody was welcome and assured plenty of sociability, fun, and possible folly.

Such socials were generally held on a large lawn for almost everyone in town came. Festoons of Japanese lanterns, swaying in the breeze, lighted the card tables with their pretty covers and chairs scattered about the lawn.

As twilight fell, people began drifting in. Pretty women in cool organdy dresses and floppy hats, men in their best suits. In the kitchen, women started cutting cakes. Luscious looking cakes with thick colored frosting. Not a mix among them. Ha! Whoever heard of a mix in those days? Women vied with each other to see who could make the lightest, tastiest, most in demand cake.

"Oh, Susie, see if you can bring me a piece of Mrs. Sanders cake, her devils food with the thick white frosting." So might one person say to one of the pretty girls in frilly aprons, with ribbons in their hair, who hurried back and forth serving big dishes of ice cream and cake. Ten cents a dish; half price for second helpings.

The gala affair of the summer, everyone who was anybody was there. The minister, his wife and children, naturally; the mayor, school superintendant. Certainly the mayor would make a speech, complimenting the women on their good work, while the women in the kitchen, wiping the perspiration from their faces with the corner of their aprons, listening, would beam. Hard work, but every woman seemed to enjoy it.

And we kids! Running around, chasing each other between tables, knocking over chairs, tromping on shrubbery, dashing into the kitchen as the crowd, thinned, hoping to get a second helping! But of everybody there, doubtless the women, counting the money they'd made after cleaning up the kitchen, got the most satisfaction of anybody. Especially if they could say, "Do you know what? We made twenty more dollars than we did last year!"

Hayrack rides on warm summer evenings came into our repertory of fun. The hayrack bedded down heavily with straw, moseying along a quiet country road behind a team of lazy horses! The moonlight, soft country air, the fragrance of new mown hay, the rustle of tasseling corn all combined to make an ideal setting for fun.

Coasting and skating are still with us. Skiing and snowmobiling have been added. But can they compete with a sleigh ride on a crisp winter night under a black sky spattered with a million glittering stars? Wrapped warm in coonskin coats and buffalo robes, with a heated soapstone at your feet; with icy winds stinging your cheeks, sleighbells tingling, runners squeaking on the hard-packed snow, what child can ever forget such an experience? Or, almost the same setting by day, with snow sparkling in the sunlight, and the anticipation of a good dinner at Grandmother's! Such are long past delights that automobiles and plowed roads have put out of the running, only to remain in the minds of those who once enjoyed them.

But a bob-sled ride on a cold moonlit winter's night is the epitome of delight. Any bunch of kids could dig up a farmer someplace willing to be hired to take them on such a ride.

Do you, by any chance, even know what a bobsled is? Just a plain old wagon box set on runners, to glide softly over the snow, where wheels might bog down and break through and tip you over. The "bob" bedded down with clean straw, with plenty of blankets to snuggle under, with high sideboards to shut off the sharp wind, was enough to keep everyone warm and happy. Generally the ride would end at somebody's house with hot chocolate, cake or cookies.

One of the boys of our bunch had a "bob", a team of mules, and an aunt who lived on a farm ten miles from town. But what were miles to a bunch of kids and a span of fleet-footed mules? We'd generally arrive at our destination around midnight. Our intended hosts, unaware of our coming, would long have been in bed, and, after a hard day's work, deep in sleep.

That made small difference to us. Cramped by our long ride, we'd climb out of the bob and pound on the door. Our host, appearing in pants and suspenders hastily pulled over his night shirt, would let us in. Soon his wife, more discreetly attired, would appear to welcome us.

The marvel is that though still half drugged with sleep, they did welcome us. With smiles and cheery greetings, they gave never a hint that they would have preferred to stay in bed. We plunked a gallon of oysters that we'd brought down on the dining room table and a box of oyster crackers. Soon a kettle of milk would be heating on the kitchen range, and while his wife busied herself in the kitchen, we helped our host pull the dining table out to its full length and put in extra leaves. As if by magic, a white table cloth would appear and the table would be set with bowls, coffee cups, and silver.

With our hostess bringing in a dish of home-made pickles, a huge platter of home-made bread, butter, and jam, filling our bowls with steaming stew – what a feast! Again joking, laughing, ribbing each other, with our host joining in as if this party were entirely his idea, it was well into the wee hours before we started for home.

Did we tarry to help clean up? To set things back in order so our genial hostess, who must rise before sunrise to get breakfast for their hungry hired men, could get back to bed? We did not! Vociferously voicing our thanks, we swarmed out of the house, scaled the sides of the bob, dropped into the soft straw, snuggled down under blankets for the long ride home.

What about our parents? Did they worry, walk the floor, fearful of what might have happened that we were so late? Doubtless not! They knew where we were going, that our mode of travel was comparatively safe. So unlike today's parents who seldom know where their children are, whom they are with, what doing, who know too well the hazards of teenagers with high-powered cars, our parents probably went to bed and to sleep, with no fear of the phone ringing to bring them tragic news, confident that a bobsled ride was as safe as any pleasure their children could indulge in.

One of the most popular forms of entertainment we went for were home talent shows. Sometimes it would be a local person who would direct such a show. Again it might be a professional – man or woman – from the big city who made a business of this sort of thing. We'd gather up whatever talent the town had to offer, which wasn't difficult as everyone wanted to be in on it, audition, choose, direct, with the result that within a remarkably short time the whole town would turn out to enjoy the performance.

One such play was <u>The Time, The Place, and The Girl</u>, a stage show then popular in New York. Though I could neither sing nor dance, I was in the chorus, about which I remember mainly we wore big floppy hats, and felt mighty important. It also instilled in us the feeling that we really could act, given the chance.

One of the most popular plays was the old fashioned minstrel show. Here again gathering up would-be actors presented no difficulties. Every man in town with a little ham in him, if he couldn't be the interlocutor[32], aspired to being an end man. Never an empty seat in the house at a home talent minstrel show. The jokes, most of them aimed at the mayor or the judge or other town bigwigs, produced gleeful laughter from the audience. The singing, dancing, banging of banjos was no less popular. It was in the minstrel shows, I believe, that the Cake Walk was introduced. A couple, strutting across the stage, bodies bent backward as far as possible, brought a round of applause when a cake was presented to the winner.

One of our most popular home talents was <u>The Bohemian Girl</u>, put on by our school music teacher, Mr. Emsley. The elite of the town performed in this. Mr. Emsley, the male lead, had a wonderful voice, and his lady-friend, a star of the show, was the town's most popular singer. My mother, with her dark brown eyes, her long hair hanging over her shoulders, made a beautiful gypsy. I vaguely remember her, gathered with others around a brilliant camp fire singing.

I, a mere chit of a child, with several other kids about my age – first or second graders – were in that show. Dressed in what I remember as Colonial costumes, though why we should have been dressed in such a manner for a gypsy play I have no idea. The important thing about that dance for me is that a good many years later I married one of the boys who had been one of the dancers. He wasn't my partner; the romance didn't begin that early!

Not all of our fun or entertainment in those days was of the do-it-yourself variety. The Willson Opera House, a plush ornate theater for so small a town, gave me hours of pleasure and probably had a part in the building of my character. Here traveling "stock companies" played, putting on a different show every night. As the leading actors generally stayed at our hotel, Dad received "comps" for all the plays and you may be sure they were never wasted. Junie and I never missed a show if we could help it.

We'd sit in the boxes if they were unoccupied, as they generally were, playing "lady." Otherwise we'd plank ourselves down in the front row, feeling very important because as guests of our hotel we knew some of the actors. Steeped in such melodramas as East Lyme, Way Down East, Uncle Tom's Cabin, Junie and I determined that when we grew up we'd be actresses. Since they stayed a week with us, I'd get to know many of the actors well. And they were as creatures from another world.

I remember one couple especially. He was a tall very thin man, she a short heavy-set woman. Rather than husband and wife, they seemed like mother and son to me, and those were indeed the roles they played in every show. One of the actresses took a fancy to me and I often visited her in her room. She'd open her trunk and show me some of her stage clothes, always glittering with sequins or otherwise ornately trimmed. She'd show me many pictures of herself in different roles, and even gave me one with her autograph.

One tragedy happened once that I was then too young to understand. A very beautiful young actress died at our hotel. I heard the help whispering about it, a whispering that suddenly stopped when I appeared on the scene. But later I learned that this young woman had fallen in love with one of the actors during the week the company played in her town, and, very much against the wishes of her parents, married him, and was in the process of becoming an actress. Unfortunately, believing herself pregnant, she had taken something to cause an abortion, which caused her death. The irony of it was that actually her belief that she was pregnant was wrong.

The opera house was also used for concerts, and once Schumann Heink played in our town. She stayed in our hotel, directly under the room in which my mother was in bed with a new baby. Mother was a great admirer of this lady because she also was the mother of a large family, a German, and a warm and loveable person. Mother had been hoping that her new baby wouldn't come before the singer arrived as she did want to go to hear her sing. But babies aren't all that accommodating in their arrival. They come when they're ready.

But Schumann Heink heard the baby cry as she was dressing for the concert, and she turned to one of our girls who was helping her (tightening her corset strings if you must know!) and asked if it was a new baby. The maid said yes, telling her how disappointed Mother was because she couldn't attend the concert. Whereupon the kindly woman folded her arms, as if cradling a baby, and sang a lullaby loud enough so that Mother could hear her. Mother never tired of telling that story, how she once heard Schumann Heink sing.

Tent shows, too, in a large tent in a wooded lot on the edge of town never failed to bring out a good share of people. As with stock companies, they stayed a week, putting on a different play each night, the same fare as we got in the opera house, but with far from the same comfort. Smoky lamps provided footlights for the improvised stage; the tent was lit by lanterns hung on poles through the tent. On hot summer nights the tent was suffocating, but so seldom did such entertainment come to our town that the tent never failed to be packed.

We had at least one carnival and one street fair each summer. The carnival was held in the same wooded lot where the tent show held forth, the street fair in an alley between the railroad tracks and the rear of business buildings. Both served about the same fare; sword swallowers, fire eaters, snake charmers, a spider girl, (an illusion done with mirrors I was told, but to this day I still don't understand how it was accomplished!), a fat woman, a giant man and wife, both over seven feet tall. The living skeleton, and did he ever look the part, skin stretched over bones you could almost see! The pleasant midgets who shook hands or chatted with anyone who wished and sold their autographed photos. The wild man from Borneo, hairy as an ape, who gobbled up a huge chunk of raw meat thrown to him through the bars of his cage, never failed to draw a crowd at feeding time. How my childish mind struggled to understand those wonders!

And sometime during the summer a merry-go-round would be set up on some vacant town lot; while ferris wheels and other rides tempted kids at the carnival. With such entertainment available the whole summer, never a child whiningly complained to Mother, "Mama, what can I do?" All we had to do was tease for the money to go there!

HOUSECLEANNG IS HARD WORK

Remember spring housecleaning? In my youth it meant general upheaval, a house was turned upside down, from cellar to attic, and its occupants given no consideration whatsoever. In the spring, the mere whisk of a wife's broom was enough to make many a husband run for cover!

Meals were cooked and eaten on the run. Furniture was piled in the center of every room. Windows were stripped of their hangings, pictures taken down from the walls, carpets ripped up from the floor.

When I say ripped, I mean just that. Literally! Wall to wall carpeting, instead of being laid in place as it is now, was tacked to the floor around the edges. To remove a carpet, each tack had to be pulled out with a small, sharp-jawed tack hammer. Undamaged tacks were dropped into a box to be re-used.

Carpets were then dragged outdoors and hung on a line to have a year's dust beaten out of them with a wire instrument called a carpet beater. The thick padding of newspaper that had been laid over the rough pine boards to protect the carpet when it was put down, and now almost pulverized by the treading of many feet, had to be swept up. The floor was scrubbed, with a stiff brush and soap and water, to a startling whiteness.

Curtains, generally of lace, were never ironed. After washing, they were hooked onto a curtain stretcher, which was much like a quilting frame, with sharp prongs around the edges on which the curtains were hooked. As several curtains could be done simultaneously, and as two or three people worked at it together, it beat ironing. The disadvantage was that the frame, supported by four chairs, had to sit in the middle of the parlor until the curtains dried.

Why every room in the house had to be turned upside down at the same time, I wondered then, I've wondered since. Perhaps, as all rooms had to be papered and painted, as long as the paraphernalia was out it was more convenient to do everything at once. To save money, many women did this work themselves. Witnessing the work of the professionals who painted and papered the hotel, my heart went out to women who took on this task.

A broom, dustpan, mop, and scrub brush was standard cleaning equipment. With these tools and a whole lot of hard work, a house could be made spotless. No modern cleansers and disinfectants were available then. Even with the windows open the smell of ammonia, turpentine, paint, wallpaper paste, and bed bug poison pervaded the house.

During housecleaning week – it generally took that long – housewives, long skirts pinned up around their waists, a towel wrapped turban style around their hair to keep the dust out of their hair, worked with a frenzy and thoroughness that might put the most assiduous Holland housewife to shame. In addition, they still had three meals a day to prepare, children to get dressed and off to school. Washing and ironing must be done. No wonder that at night they dropped into bed like a lump of lead on a plummet!

Putting a house back in order was almost as torturous as tearing it apart. Carpets had to be relaid – women, and often children, crawling along on hands and knees pounding tacks with their miniature hammers. Pictures and curtains must be rehung, dishes put back in freshly painted cupboards. Beds must be reassembled, heavy furniture returned to its original spot. Woe to that housewife who had a penchant for changing things around, causing a considerate husband, coming quietly in the dark so as not to waken his weary wife, to find himself crashing to the floor, rather than the bed he aimed for!

But when all was done, the house gleamed like a freshly cut diamond, and hard work and aching bones were forgotten in the satisfaction gained. And the husband, who hadn't so much as pounded a tack, or laid a beater against a carpet, puffed himself up as if he'd been the doer!

Our hotel also suffered the ordeal of spring housecleaning. Fortunately, however, no more than two rooms were done at a time. Still, this was a job and Mother worked right along with the help. Ripping up carpets, sending them out to the line to be beaten. Airing mattresses too.

Carpets then came in strips, about a yard wide, purchased by the yard. Strips had to be sewn together with a strong needle and heavy carpet thread, which was generally run over a hunk of beeswax so it could be pulled through the heavy carpeting more easily. Sometimes the threads would be so worn that a carpet had to be resewn. Should a carpet show much wear in the middle, Mother would rip it apart, and sew the outsides together, so the weak part would be around the edge. Or sometimes she'd move the position of the bed to cover a weak spot in the carpeting.

Though I was too young to help with that, I liked to help tack down the carpet so much that I'd hurry home from school to do it. For that we used a carpet stretcher, a row of stout teeth at the end of a mop handle. If a carpet seemed to have shrunk, we'd set those teeth against it and push until the edges met the wall. While someone pushed, another person would put in tacks every so far apart. What I liked to do was pound the tacks in between spaces.

What Mother insisted on doing herself was painting the beds with bed-bug poison. Our hotel had the reputation of being bed-bug free. She meant to keep it so. This poison was an evil smelling liquid that would keep the devil himself away! We bought it from the drugstore in a brown glass gallon jug. Mother would pour some in a bowl, dip in her brush, and go over every inch of a bed and springs, making sure she got in every crack. If Mother superintended the cleaning of a room you could be sure is was clean!

Another of her tasks in those early hotel days was the making of sheets. Sheets didn't come already made, sheeting came by the bolt. It had to be torn into the right lengths and hemmed; the same for pillow case tubing. For a hotel of fifty rooms, this was no small job. But Mother would make fun of it.

She'd have a sheeting "bee". Several of the help, between their other jobs, would gather in her room. Some would tear the sheeting into the right lengths, others man the machine. Sewing machines then apparently were not equipped with hemmers, for the girls would press the hems in with their fingers, before turning them over to the seamstress.

It was the same with table linens. Both tablecloth and napkins came by the bolt. Even as a child, I helped press the napkin hems into place. Always there'd be fun and laughter. Mother might send down to the kitchen for fruit or something to snack on. The task might take several days, but when done the linen closet shelves would groan under a supply of new linens.

The bedding was of the best muslin; the table linen of the finest damask—a quality I'd not mind having in my home today. Mother was always one for buying the best. She said it lasted longer.

Mother found it increasingly hard to rear so many lively children and keep them quiet in the confines of a few hotel rooms. They needed a yard to run, romp, and yell in. So while some of the children were still small, and Mother kept having babies, though Dad continued to run the hotel, we moved into a private home.

Mother hired a maid when possible. But few girls cared to work in a family with so many children. It was then that I, young as I was, learned how true was a slogan of that day: "A man's work is from sun to sun. A woman's work is never done." How often my mother worked at night, even to scrubbing the kitchen floor, after we children were in bed, asleep!

For aside from spring cleaning, the ardors of woman's every day work was long and hard, mainly because of her primitive equipment. Brooms, dust pan, mop and pail, scrub brush, wash board! Torture tools.

Take sweeping—every room in a house! Sweeping raised dust. To keep it down some women spread dampened shredded newspaper over a carpet before going after it with a broom. Others used coarse salt. Commercial sweeping powders cost money. As one woman I knew said, she looked long and hard at a dollar before spending it. A sum we'd spend today more thoughtlessly than we'd spend a dime then.

A kitchen floor was a woman's bête noir.[33] Most floors were of white pine which feet had a habit of wearing into shallow hollows where they trod oftenest. Before sink, stove, table, doorways! As a woman was judged by the whiteness of her floor, a stiff scrub brush, soap, water and often lye were in constant use to keep it so.

When congoleum rugs appeared, women fell for them like leaves from trees in autumn. Fancied up with a pretty pattern, they looked beautiful when new. But feet wore them, too. Down to an ugly brown base, gradually through to the floor. Also the rough boards underneath wore through, making long brown streaks across the room. Much time passed before congoleum with its all-the-way-through pattern, came into being.

The shininess of her kitchen range was another criteria of a woman's housekeeping. To keep it black and shiny she polished it with a black paste, the result of which made both her stove and her heart glow. But such paste smudged the bottom of her pots and pans, which in turn smudged whatever she set them on.

Since stoves must be fed as well as have ashes removed, they were work. Soft coal was the fuel used in Iowa, which a woman had to run down cellar to get. Wood, a rare commodity, was used mostly for building. If, to hasten cooking, a utensil was set down directly over the flames, it's bottom became so sooty that only the inside was washed. Since the soot would dirty attractive shelf paper with its dainty over-hanging edge, sooty utensils were hung in the cellar-way or under the enclosed sink.

Cleaning products were poor. Many soaps faded clothes. My mother used a large, irregular-shaped, unwrapped bar which she bought by the case. Farm women, having plenty of lard, sometimes made their own soap, a product frequently better than any they could buy.

Clothing materials, unfortunately, were seldom fade-proof. Soaking them in a solution of salt and vinegar helped solve that problem. Such treated materials had to be ironed before they could be used.

A plastic tablecloth? Ha! Oilcloth was the piece de resistance. It came in wide widths, in many attractive patterns and colors. A new oilcloth on the kitchen table was as delightful as a new plastic cover today. Some women tacked the oilcloth on, leaving no loose edges. Others let it hang loose. Whichever way, on edges, corners, places of wear, the oilcloth would crack and peel, leaving an unsightly brown base. To avoid this, my mother had her kitchen table covered with zinc.

A yellow cleaning powder did not live up to the promise of the energetic Gold Dust Twins pictured on the box. Especially in the hard water brewed in Iowa. As to window cleaners, Sapolia, a hard white bar, reigned supreme. It covered the window with a white film when you washed with it, which when wiped away left a window sparkling clean. It also left a white dust on the sill, which had to be washed off.

A brick with a knife beside it had a permanent place on a corner of Mother's sink. When a pot or pan needed scouring, she'd shave powder onto it from the brick. It worked, but how much easier it would have been to shake powder out of a can, had she had such a thing. As a forerunner of today's many wonderful scouring pads, women then had a gadget made of a series of small intertwined steel rings. Ingenious, but not too effective.

I don't recall any polish such as waxes or oils. Women used a feather duster, a fluff of feathers attached to a handle with which they flicked dust off chairs, table, pianos; not getting rid of it, mind you, merely displacing it until it found a safer place to settle. One thing for sure. No woman was troubled by a Fuller brush man. Nor a Stanley agent begging her to give a party. They were still a long way into the future.

Monday was washday! No getting around that. Women of Mother's day would no more think of letting Monday pass without doing family wash, than letting their children go without their Saturday night bath.

How memories of those Saturday nights come rushing back. One kid after another into the tub, Mother lifting them out, dripping, setting them up on the stool to dry them, slipping them into a night gown, sending them up to bed. No Saturday night celebrations for Mother!

I can see Mother yet, in those years we lived in a private home, standing in the middle of the kitchen sorting clothes. White in one pile, light colored in another, in the third real dark and dirty articles. When sorted, she'd dump each pile into a separate tub, fill it with water, pour in whatever water softener she used, to let them soak overnight. This she did every Sunday night without fail, so clothes would be ready for washing bright and early Monday morning. Because of Iowa's hard water, soaking and washing powder were necessary, unless you wished your clothes to come out that horrible tattle-tale grey.

The fortunate had a cistern to catch the rain water from the roof. A rain barrel, set under an eaves spout, served the same function. Such soft water was invaluable for getting clothes clean and white sans benefit of softener; wonderful for washing hair!

Mother's washing machine was wooden, with a dolly that had to be whirled by a wheel turned by hand. This job, done by us girls, caused many an argument. How we'd watch to make sure each girl did her quota of turns, twenty-five, thirty! How we'd argue as to whose turn was next! "I did it last time." "I've done it twice, you only once." How quickly we'd release that wheel when Mother decided clothes were washed enough! But there'd be another tubful, and another.

Clothes still had to be wrung through the wringer by hand, carried to the boiler on the stove. Mother had to rise early to fill that boiler, and build a brisk fire under it, to make sure the water was boiling when needed. Every good housewife boiled her clothes to keep them white! Clothes then had to be ladled out of the boiling hot water with a wash stick – generally a sawed off broom stick, wrung into blueing water, then again into clear water, finally, they were hung up to dry.

And was Mother most fastidious about that! Matching socks had to be hung together. Towels, pillow cases, napkins, diapers, (We always had diapers!) were hung in orderly array, as were sheets and table cloths.

Washing done, the machine was pushed out on to the back porch to await next Monday. A little water was always left in, otherwise, the wood would dry out, so when next filled, water would spout from every shrunken crack. When this happened an argument would ensue. Who was to blame? The one who'd put the machine away and forgotten to leave some water in.

A wash boiler was an important commodity. All copper, if one could afford it. If not, the boiler must at least have a copper bottom. Necessary not only for boiling clothes, but also for canning. Beans, peas, meat, corn, packed in glass jars and set in the boiler, must be boiled briskly for four hours. No freezing foods then! At farm sales or at threshing time in the Midwest, when many men had to be fed, coffee was made in a boiler. Kept on the stove for hours, it often became strong enough to stand alone. <u>And bitter</u>!

I have seen Mother standing at the kitchen table dampening clothes she had just taken from the line, <u>dry</u>! (Seems silly, doesn't it?) She'd then roll them into tight little bundles, pack them away in a huge clothes basket, cover them, and set them aside for the next day's ironing.

Compared to today's scant wearing apparel, that scarcely needs the touch of an iron, yesterday's ironing was a Herculean task. Long skirts were worn over two or three petticoats. Sleeves were long, necks high. The only visible part of a woman's body was her face and hands. And every garment not only frothed with ruffles, but needed to be starched. Even table linens, slightly, to give them body.

And table linens were <u>used.</u> A hostess who offered a guest a paper napkin, had such an item existed, would have been scorned. Mother used white table cloths and napkins, with napkin rings. For our large family, napkins were many, table cloths long. Table linens alone made Mother's ironing enormous. Not to mention those ruffled garments for seven daughters! Needless to say, we all learned to iron early!

And our irons! Electric? Ha! Don't be funny! Heavy triangles of solid iron with handles attached, heated on a red hot stove. You've probably seen them; today we use them as doorstops! Working in torrid weather in such a heated kitchen was punishment enough. Pushing a heavy iron back and forth, sliding its point into every ruffle, was gruesome. Perspiration dropping from a woman's brow could dampen her clothes enough! As one iron cooled, it was returned to the stove and a hot one was picked up. It was years before electric irons hit the market to lighten a woman's ironing. Longer yet, before women's clothing shrunk to today's minimum, and materials that need no ironing were invented!

"WASTE NOT, WANT NOT"

I was born in an era when "save" was the most important word in the dictionary. Maybe even the most important word in the Bible. (Although the Bible deals mainly with saving souls!) "Waste not, want not," "Willful waste makes woeful want," were the dictums of my childhood.

My mother was a saver of the first water. And high on her list of things to be saved was bread, the staff of life. Throwing away bread was a sin. The only permissible way was to "Cast your bread upon the waters." Trouble was, my mother didn't live near any "waters!" She used up her old bread by cooking it with tomatoes, in making bread pudding, for dressing, or as crumbs, which had any number of uses.

The real symbol of my mother's saving complex (though complex was then a word so seldom heard that you had to reach for a dictionary if you ever ran across it in your reading!) were her five piece bags. Large, commodious, bulging, made of striped ticking or blue denim, they hung by heavy drawstrings on strong hooks at the foot of the back stairway. There was a bag each for satin, silk, linen, cotton, and one for the trimmings, like laces, braids, embroideries, or velvets. For just as with bread in our home, so not a scrap of material was thrown away until the last inch of use had been wrung from it.

Some women with an artistic bent would cut up old dresses, and odds and ends of materials to make crazy quilts. They'd cut them into squares, circle, triangles, half-moons, and fasten them together with intricate feather-stitching. They were well named. Crazy! They looked the part and you'd have thought it would have made the woman who fashioned them just that!

But they were a matter for pride in any home. Laid out on the couch for all to see, they were a conversation piece deluxe. The scraps from Uncle Joe's neckties, the velvet trimming off Aunt Lucy's go-to-meeting gown, scraps left from sister's wedding dress, provided not only work for otherwise idle fingers, but brought back many happy memories as years passed. Sometimes they were even used to keep people warm!

Crazy quilts were not the fashion in our house. There every scrap of material was converted into clothing. Once a garment was outgrown, out-moded or worn out, it was ripped apart, seam by seam, with a real razor. The kind one could cut his throat, as well as shave, with, were he so disposed. Often we children were conscripted to help with this ripping, a task we didn't relish. Not only was it a tedious job, but woe betide the child who cut into the material, rather than sever the threads that held it together!

Once these garments were in pieces, (and believe me, there were many pieces, for garments then were many-gored, many seamed, much ruffled and pleated) the material was washed, ironed or steamed, similar materials were rolled together, tied, and dropped into their respective bags to await reincarnation.

For this purpose, each spring and fall a seamstress would come to our home and for several weeks the whirr of the foot-treadle machine would be heard throughout the house. The making of one's clothes, or the hiring of a seamstress, was a necessity. Ready-made or store-bought clothes were practically unknown. It was a day when the professional dressmaker flourished.

I smile now when I think back to a certain Easter. Each of us girls was wearing a dress made over from a dress of her next oldest sister. Being the oldest, I often got a dress made from new material, but this day I was wearing made-over finery of my mother's. A fact that bothered me not at all, since Mother always had lovely clothes.

It's possible that my small brother may have been wearing a suit made from one of my father's. Or even a velvet Little Lord Fauntleroy suit made from a dress of Mother's, though he was as far from being a Little Lord Fauntleroy as any child I can imagine!

Were we humiliated by this hand-me-down finery? Did we cringe, shrink back into our shells, or develop an inferiority complex? Believe you me, no!

We spread our tails and strutted around like vain-glorious peacocks. We bragged to whomever would listen that I was wearing a made-over dress of Mother's that my next younger sister was wearing a dress that had been mine, and so on down the list.

We had reason to brag. Anything made under Mother's supervision (she was once a professional seamstress herself) was sure to pass muster. Mother loved pretty clothes. She delighted in delicate laces, dainty embroideries, ruffles, ribbons, and she used them abundantly on our clothes. I'm sure that on Easter we must have been wearing wide, silk ribbon sashes tied with a bib bow in back. Mother doted on sashes, and those were possibly the one article of our finery that was absolutely new.

Clothes weren't the only things people recycled. Nobody, back then, ever threw anything away. Houses

113

had commodious attics and up to the attic went anything unneeded or unwanted. To spend the rest of their lives there, probably, but, hopefully, to stay there until someone could find use for the thing.

That's how a lot of newlyweds got half their furniture. Kids didn't furnish their homes with everything new as they do today. You see, buying on the installment plan was then unknown. Things could be charged, but that wasn't much help; they had to be paid for at the end of the month. A couple would probably have enough money to buy their stove (every woman wanted a new stove since it was generally the thing in her house of which she was most proud!) and a bed, since that was a necessity. They'd probably have enough, too, for a kitchen table and chairs.

But they'd take anything else that anyone would give them. If it was broken, they'd mend it, paint it. An old fashioned bureau that had belonged to Aunt Kitty, a lounge, which probably needed reupholstering, that had belonged to Grandpa Nelson. An old fashioned clock that didn't work, but it had been in the family for years and possibly could be fixed. Thus, piece by piece, a young couple might furnish their home until they made enough money to buy new. Then they could put the old furniture up in their attic, where it would stay until they could pass it on to someone else in need. That way, things got used right down to the very bone!

AT THE STORE

Going shopping was an activity I considered exciting, so whenever I had the chance, I would either accompany someone else or go alone to the shops in our town. Since we lived in a hotel, I wasn't sent to the store to get groceries, as were some of my friends, but I'd often go with Junie, carrying a shiny tin pail, to a small dairy shop a block from her home for milk. The man would fill her pail from a big pitcher, then clamp the lid on tight. A nickel a quart! She might also get bread there, unwrapped. Whether or not the man's hands were clean, he'd grab up a loaf of bread and stuff it into a bag. The bread too was only a nickel.

Sometimes I'd go with another friend to the butter and egg store. The man would dig a hunk of butter out of a big tub with a wooden ladle, slap it down on a piece of paper on the scales, then wrap it. Since this friend was from a large family with limited resources, her mother always bought cracked eggs which were cheaper. The man would put them in a bag, not a box;

which isn't even a good carrier for whole eggs! We'd get to fooling on the way to her house, and frequently by the time we handed the eggs over to her mother, the bag was dripping with sticky egg white.

I liked to go with Junie when she paid her mother's grocery bills. The storekeeper always gave her candy in a small striped bag, and she'd share it with me on the way home.

The butcher was a good friend of mine. I can remember his shop so well. The floor was carpeted with a thick layer of clean yellow sawdust. Behind the counter stood the butcher, wielding his shiny cleaver over a much scarred chopping block. From heavy ceiling hooks along one wall hung a row of bloody carcasses of pork, beef, lamb, mutton. When a customer came in, the butcher would take his order, then take a carcass off the hook, fling it over one shoulder, and carry it to the chopping block where he'd cut off a piece of meat, according to the customer's order.

This butcher was the father of one of my schoolmates. In fact, there was hardly a merchant in town who wasn't the father of one of my schoolmates, which made shopping so much nicer! I could bounce into his store any time I wanted and ask for a ring of bologna and get it. He'd lift it down from a hook above the counter and hand it over. Free! A ring of bologna only cost five cents back then, and I'm sure the butcher's willingness to give it to me had a lot to do with the fact that Dad bought the meat for the hotel at that shop!

There was one store that I didn't like to visit. It wasn't in our town, but it was near a farm where I often went to see a friend. It was a real country store, the only place to get groceries in the small whistle-stop town. My friend's mother would get in their spring wagon to go to town to shop, and we'd go along with her for the ride.

Though I was too young to let it bother me, it was the dreariest store I've <u>ever</u> been in. Small, dingy, fly-specked! Flies crawling over uncovered food! It reeked of smoke from cheap tobacco coming from the corncob pipes of the roughly-clad men gathered around the pot-bellied stove in the middle of the store. A good hang-out for idlers!

Nothing in that store came in fancy-wrapped packages or bottles, nor from attractively arranged shelves. Everything that could came in bulk. Crackers came in a big barrel set by the door from which passers-by could help themselves and generally did. They might also help themselves to a big slice of cheese from the big uncovered round on the counter, if the  grocer's attention happened to be directed elsewhere.

Beans - kidney, yellow-eye, or navy, coffee, sugar, brown or white, rice, split peas, rolled oats, and other cereals; these were all in covered wooden bins that hung from the long, dark, scarred counter. The grocer ladled out the number of pounds a customer wanted into the battered tin basket of a counter scales, and dumped it into a bag to be carried home.

But what I really liked best was to go shopping with my mother. For she knew everybody in town and going shopping was almost like going visiting. Shopping was leisurely in those days. There were stools in front of the counters for the customers to sit on. Little round ones like the old fashioned piano stools that would go round and round if you wanted them to.

When buying dress material, Mother would sit on a stool, tell the clerk what she wanted, and she would bring out bolt after bolt of beautiful materials. Silks, satins, moiré if it were winter. Mother loved moiré. If it were summer, beautiful dimities, lawns, and organdy of which Mother was especially fond. She'd take the material between her fingers to test its texture, and hold it so she got the right light on it to examine its color. Maybe she wouldn't make up her mind right then, and would prefer to think about it for awhile. Or, maybe she knew exactly what she wanted and would buy it. The clerk would measure the material, using the "yardstick" that was on the edge of the counter.

I liked it best when Mother looked through the big books of laces, trimmings, and embroideries. Mother went for any kind of trimming. And, ribbons! Gold, silver, different kinds of braids. She loved to use a lot of embroidery on the clothes of us girls. We even made our own underwear then. About the only things you could buy ready-made were coats and long winter knit underwear. Ladies wore underpants that came to their knees and were gathered in at the bottom and edged with ruffles of lace or embroideries. Children's underpants were made in much the same way. Ladies also wore corset covers, generally with several rows of full ruffles or embroidery across the front. They'd starch them very stiff to make their blouses stick out.

Mother always spent a long time over trimming books. Then she'd point out to the clerk the things she wanted, the clerk would take bolts of whatever it was from the shelves and measure out Mother's order. Mother always had such a time making up her mind that she'd take two or three kinds when she only needed one. I used to get tired waiting for her to make up her mind and I'd swing myself around and around on one of the stools until she would tell me to quit. I made her nervous.

Most of our dry goods shopping was done at Wheeler's store. The Wheelers were among the town's earliest settlers, and, in the real early days Mrs. Wheeler had a school in the back of her store where she taught the children.

When I knew the Wheelers they were elderly. Older than my parents, but Mother and Mrs. Wheeler were good friends. Although they had their own apartment over their store, they took all their meals at our hotel. Their table was right next to ours and Mrs. Wheeler and Mother would talk back and forth. Having no children of her own, Mrs. Wheeler loved us kids and was nice to all of us.

The Wheeler's store was another place I used to go when I couldn't find anything else to do. They had one clerk; her name was Marion. Marion would let me come behind the counter with her and really play store!

The Wheeler's were both short and – well, I suppose you'd say chubby. Mr. Wheeler's hair was grey but Mrs. Wheeler's was mostly black, and she had friendly, merry eyes. They both were friendly and jolly, which is why people continued to trade with them when a larger and fancier store opened up in town.

Mrs. Wheeler both painted and taught china painting. Mother was one of her best students. As a result, we had lots of lovely pieces of her handiwork in out suite.

Another place I loved to go with Mother was to Amanda Johnson's when she wanted to buy a hat or have one made. I don't remember when Miss Johnson wasn't in that same little shop. She was a big, well-upholstered woman. Her hair was very white and made a soft frame around her face. Although she seemed very old to me, her skin was as smooth as silk. But then, once it was in our local newspaper, in big black headlines, "Amanda Johnson Hasn't Washed Her Face In Twenty Years." Believe it or not, that was the truth, the whole truth! She cleaned her face with cold cream, soap and water never touch it!

The small curtained off alcove at the rear of her shop was a fascinating place to me. There were boxes and boxes of feathers, whole birds, ribbons, silks, satins, velvets. And flowers! Every kind of flower you could imagine. She generally had two girls working back there, and I'd sit and watch them make hats. Making new hats from old, or taking just a plain straw hat, and, with flowers and ribbons, turning it into a woman's dream. Mother, who always wanted her hats little, had some beautiful hats made for her at Miss Johnson's shop.

Then there was Miss Skewis, the dressmaker. Miss Skewis was just as tiny and skinny as Miss Johnson was opposite. And a real spinster! Instead of being called a dressmaker, I presume that today – considering what she could do with a few yards of material – she'd be considered a fashion designer! I used to love to go with Mother when she'd go to try on dresses Miss Skewis was making for her. She had a low platform that she had people stand on when they were trying things on. And Miss Skewis always had a mouthful of pins that she would use when pinning up a hem or taking in a seam.

Sometimes Miss Skewis would take absolutely new material, drape it around Mother, pin it into place, then cut the material then and there. She knew just how to do it, and everything she made was beautiful. The most important women in town came to her to have their dresses made. She had several girls working for her at a long table in the back room, and you could always hear the sound of a foot treadle machine whirring.

If I got tired of watching her fit Mother, I'd go through her fashion journals. If she had any old ones, she'd let me have them for paper dolls. I played with paper dolls more than with real ones. I'd have whole families, mother, father, children, aunts, uncles, and all with extensive wardrobes. I kept them in different pages of a big book. Junie did the same with hers, and when we'd get together we'd play with our paper dolls by the hour. For my male paper dolls, I'd go to the tailor who made my father's suits and ask for their old fashion journals. I always had a terrible time keeping my younger sisters out of my paper dolls, and no matter where I hid them in the hotel, they'd find them there.

Mrs. Murphy, a widow and the mother of one of my schoolmates, generally made my clothes. I didn't mind standing for her so much, because when I got tired she'd let me sit down. But when occasionally Mother had Miss Skewis make something for me, she'd keep me standing so long! I'd fidget, then she'd get impatient and tell me to stand still.

Mother later found a sewing woman who would come for a few weeks each spring and fall to get us kids outfitted. When you consider that we couldn't get anything ready-made, it took a lot of sewing for so many girls. By today's standards it didn't take too much money, although it might have been a lot then. The sewing woman came so often she was like one of the family and only received a dollar a day!

GOOD FOR WHAT AILS YOU

As I took a spoonful of cough medicine recently and discovered I liked it, my mind flew back to my childhood when I so loved Castoria (a regular medicine in our home) that one day I sneaked a bottle of it out of the medicine chest, crawled under the bed, and drained the bottle dry. A small bottle! But my mother, horrified when she learned what I'd done, frantically phoned dear old Doctor Whitley to find out what to do. The remedy was not pleasant. An emetic![34] But, then, punishment for pleasure wrongly attained is never pleasant!

Memories of this brought memories of that good doctor and how much we children all loved him. He was almost like one of the family, and I could almost say we were glad when one of us were sick, so he could be sent for.

He officiated at the birth of 11 of my mother's twelve children. I, the oldest, was born before we moved to Iowa. But though I was not one of his "children" I felt as important as if I were, as he attended to all my ills.

He was our family doctor from before I can remember until well after I was married. Yet from the first day I saw him to the last, he always looked the same. He never seemed to age. Perhaps that was because of his neatly trimmed beard which so hid his face it never seemed to change.

I can still see him coming into my mother's hotel room carrying that little black bag. A bag in which I once believed he brought her babies. Later I learned that the stork was the donor. I can still see him open that little bag on Mother's small bedroom stand, disclosing those neat rows of little glass bottles, each carrying its own magic potion, which I always regarded curiously. Breathlessly we children watched as he poured powders from those bottles into small squares of white paper, then folded it neatly in.

But before he left he'd ask for a half glass of water, pour into it contents of one of those papers, lay a spoon over the top of the glass. Fever medicine, he called it, and instructed my mother to give the patient a spoonful every so often.

Whenever anything drastic happened in our house, Mother's first words were apt to be, "go call Dr. Whitley." So one of us kids would rush down to the office and relay the message to my father or the clerk. It might seem he had no other patients than us, for scarcely was the message conveyed than, like a genii when the lamp is rubbed, he'd appear. Which was understandable, as his office was right across the street from the hotel.

I liked to go to his office with Mother. A large, square, high-ceilinged room over the corner drug store, walled on two sides with tall windows, it was plainly furnished with a large desk and a few chairs. After Dr. Whitley had diagnosed the ailment, he'd disappear into a small alcove portioned off in one corner of his office. When he reappeared, he'd be carrying a bottle of ugly brown medicine or a box of pills. Never once did he send us away with a prescription to be filled at the drug store just below him. He doled out his own medicine.

As I grew older I was allowed to go to the doctor alone. Then as he probed me with questions regarding my ailment, I'd feel very grown-up, being on my own. He had no office girl. No one to whom I had to give my name, age, place of birth, list of childhood diseases, names of my parents, grandparents, how old they had lived, what illnesses they had had, what they died of. Why should I? He knew our family history almost as well as he knew his own!

No Blue Cross, Blue Shield, Medicare, or what have you existed in those days, yet I'm sure my father never paid a doctor bill. Not outright anyway! He and the doctor had a system that worked perfectly for both. In return for services rendered, every Sunday, holiday, or whenever he felt like it, the Whitley family, (five in all – a girl my age and a friend of mine) bringing whatever guests they wished, came to the hotel for dinner. I doubt if either my father or the doctor knew what each owed the other, or made out a bill. This seemed a fair and easy way to square their indebtedness.

Mother had a lot of things that were good for illness too. On her dresser she kept a decanter of whiskey, or brandy, mixed with rock candy. This was strictly for colds and sore throats. But, my goodness, it was on par with Castoria with me! How I wished I could have it oftener! Coughing, pretending I had a cold did no good. I couldn't fool Mother. Only an emergency removed the stopper from that decanter. Then Mother dealt it out by stingy spoonfuls.

Mother was great for old fashioned remedies, the kind she'd been brought up on. For one of them I had no love whatsoever. Sulphur and molasses! It was horrible. Supposedly a blood thinner of our thick winter's blood, it was a spring tonic. We kids had to take it three days in a row, skip three days, take it again for three days until all told we'd taken nine doses when our agony ended. I can still see us kids lined up at the foot of Mother's bed, laughing at the fuss the ones ahead of us made, but making horrible faces when it came our turn.

One of Mother's mixtures I never fussed against was senna tea leaves and figs. She'd mold it into small bars and cut off our dosage. Doled out sparingly, its action was never severe. But those small doses were mere samples, creating a yen for more.

Once when our parents went to hot Springs Arkansas for Dad's rheumatism, as we then called arthritis, she forgot to tell the nursemaid in whose care she left us about our daily doses. But I didn't forget. She kept it in a hand painted covered bowl on her mantel, and I helped myself daily to however much I wanted. Our nurse finally discovered what was going on and put a stop to my eating.

Vermifuge was another remedy that we were given on occasion. Apparently the first thing an adult thought of when a child grew cranky, irritable, or out of sorts was, "She must have worms." Let a child throw a tantrum, go off her feed, run a fever, then came the dictum, "Worms," and down came the vermifuge bottle and spoon.

I remember when I had lung fever or, as we would call it today, pneumonia. The treatment was long and painful: hot flaxseed poultices applied regularly to the chest. I have vague recollections of a steaming vessel near my bed, in which the poultices were heated, and a white-clad nurse in attendance. I remember hushed voices, a darkened room, and the nurse and my mother hovering over me changing poultices.

Whoever hears of flaxseed poultices today? For that matter, how about rock candy and whiskey, vermifuge, or castoria? Although these remedies are considered primitive today, they did their job then, and helped keep us alive.

IN MY YOUNG LIFE

Looking back on my childhood, I am aware of the many things that happened outside of our town that figured into our life. These events, both scientific and political, have great historical significance. But, as a child, I measured their importance only by the effect they had on me and my world.

I remember that when the first telephone was put in our hotel it was such an unbelievable miracle that a small circle of onlookers gathered to watch it being installed. It was a strange looking gadget. Just an oak panel, less than a yard long, with a box at the top, that hung on the wall. Two bells were at the top of the box, below them a spout into which one spoke, which could be moved up or down according to the height of the speaker.

An odd-looking contraption, certainly! But, oh the wonders of it! Now a man need not ride wildly, for miles, on horseback, to get a doctor for his wife about to have a baby. He need only speak into this instrument; the doctor would come. The work, worry, time it was to save!

As the men picked up their tools to depart, someone suggested that I be the first to speak over it, and as they brought a box for me to stand on, I grew all excited. Someone showed me how to turn the crank, lift the receiver. I didn't even have to give a number. All I needed to say when a voice answered was, "Give me Oppenheimer's house, please." When Junie answered I could hardly believe my ears. What we talked about, how long, I've forgotten. Never will I forget my wonder, as I stepped down off that box, that I had just talked to my best friend several blocks away!

Doubtless we were given numbers to call, but they were ignored. We merely asked for whom we wanted. Eames' grocery store, the meat market, or whoever. It was years before the "operator" replaced "central", or we were required to give the operator a number.

It was an exciting day when I stood at the curb beside my mother and watched our town boys march off to the Spanish-American war. No uniforms, just an array of nondescript garments. A marching band behind them played "When Johnny Comes Marching Home Again." The streets were lined with people waving their hats, cheering them on. But there were mothers there too, with tears in their eyes.

That was the war, remember, that begat the slogan "Remember The Maine." Another war, according to some historians, that never should have been. The Battleship Maine was sunk by an explosion, all right, but whether by an explosion from inside or out was never determined. And the Spanish had conceded all we'd asked. President McKinley was against fighting. A couple of Washington bigwigs, however, though we should fight and talked McKinley into it. So we Americans whipped our emotions into high with "Remember The Maine," and went to war.

But that's not why I remember the Maine. Suddenly, as the boys marched by, my mother, my beautiful mother, stepped from the curb, and long skirts trailing in the dust, rushed out to kiss one of the marching boys. I was horrified, my childish heart shocked that my mother would kiss any man but my father. As she stepped back on the curb I said, "Mother, you shouldn't have done that."

But what a kind thing she had done! It was Archie, our porter or man of all trades. It wasn't only because he worked for us that impelled Mother to rush out into the streets and kiss him. She knew Archie was an orphan, that he and his brother Bill (our day clerk) had been reared in an orphanage, so Archie had no one else to kiss him goodbye. To care whether he went off to war, or if he came back. Not even a girl, as far as Mother knew.

The war was short, with few casualties. Within months the band that had played "When Johnny Comes Marching Home" was playing tunes to welcome them back. Of the 400,000 volunteers (Notice, please, volunteers; no conscription then. Patriotism ran high. Boys rushed to the aid of their country when it needed them.) 379 died on the battlefield or of mortal wounds. Our big losses resulted from lack of sanitation in army camps. For every man who died in battle, thirteen died of disease or fever.

Archie was one of the lucky ones: he came home. He wrestled with trunks and sample cases for years after that. And whenever Mother spoke of him, or Bill, she'd say that no finer boys ever worked for us.

One day my mother sent me across the street to the milliner's for a hat she'd had retrimmed. In those days women possessed a trait most folks seem to have outgrown called thrift. Instead of buying a new hat, they'd have an old one made over. And this milliner was just the one to do it. She'd turn an old hat front side back, upside down, replace flowers with feathers, perk up with velvets or ribbons.

Junie was with me that day, but the moment we stepped inside that shop we forgot about hats, for Miss Johnson, a heavy, white-haired woman said, "Isn't it terrible! President McKinley has been shot!"

I can't recall that the news particularly stunned me. My main reaction, as I accepted the hat I'd come for, was to rush back to the hotel and tell my father. But to our surprise, that's what the men in the office were already discussing when we got there. No radio, no TV! No boys on the street calling "Extra, Extra!" This was before the invention of long distance telephoning, so only by telegraph could that news have come all the way to our town.

I wasn't overly impressed when President Taft visited Webster City. But it was a great day for our Republican town, and they paid homage to this Republican President. Crowds were on the street, cheering, waving their hats. Though I had never seen a president before, to me he was merely a red-faced fat man riding up and down our main street, waving his hat, smiling and nodding first to one side of the street, then the other.

Everyone in town flocked to see our first movie. It was held under a leaky canvas roof, supported by unsteady poles, in a vacant lot on the main street of our town. Seats were planks set on upturned tiles.

The lot was a few steps down from the sidewalk. When it rained the canvas roof leaked and water gushing down the street turned the ground to a mixture of mud and soggy tangled grass. And it rained the night of the first movie! Yet because this was a first, no one let the rain keep them away.

The picture, shown on what was little more that a sheet stretched across the front of the tent (If this covering could be dignified by the name of tent!) was dark, the actor's movements jerky, and, of course, it was silent. Who the actors were, or if some of them later rose to fame, I don't know. Nor do I remember what the picture was about. I was on my first date with the most popular boy in school, and so conscious of his hand lightly encircling my arm, that many details of this great event I failed to notice!

This tent was our movie "theater" for several summers. Eventually we fell heir to a real theater in a long brick building. Movies could now be shown year round. It was called a Nickelodeon. Admission, one nickel!

This building had once been a harness shop, and as a movie theater it was, to our small town, pretentious. The large, well-lighted lobby, fronted by a wide plate glass window with a ticket booth in the center, was adorned with large palms. The darkened theater with comfortable folding chairs instead of planks for seats, with music by a real organist setting the mood, was relaxing.

Its first picture, in which the acting had greatly improved over that of the earlier movies, was a Civil War Epic. In one scene, four or six horses, pulling heavy artillery, slid down one steep bank, splashed through a river, and climbed up another bank. At its end, the picture, just for kicks, was run backwards. The sight of those horses running backwards, pushing the artillery back through the river, up the other bank, set the whole theater to roaring!

Shows were continuous. You could come at the beginning, middle, or end and stay as long as you wished, seeing the first part after you'd seen the end. It was customary then, too, to have a singer take the stage between shows. The words of his songs were shown on the screen so the audience could sing right along with him. Leaving the theater after a show like that, you really felt as if you'd had your nickel's worth!

Another event I remember, although it is of no great historical significance, is quite amusing in the re-telling. It is the great kissing bug scare we had one summer when I was a child. The kissing bug was said to be a bug that came out only at night. It bit people on the lips as they slept and its sting was lethal. The disastrous thing about it was, it could cut its way through any screen. So everyone was sleeping with their windows closed, sweltering in that hot humid Iowa heat that makes farmers smile because "You can almost hear the corn grow."

No one had ever seen a kissing bug! They'd just heard of people being bitten, and dying. Never anyone they knew! So one day when our yardman came to me and asked if I wanted to see a dead kissing bug, I jumped at the chance and grabbed for the folded paper he held out to me.

When I unfolded that paper, I let out a scream. Whatever was supposed to be dead in that paper flew up in my face! I dropped the paper, looked down at the thing that had fallen on the floor. It was a couple of sticks! They'd been so wound together with a rubber band that when the paper was unfolded, the band let loose, and let the sticks fly. Was I ever mad! "I could have died of a heart attack," I stormed at George.

Fear of the kissing bug gradually died. No one ever knew anyone who'd been kissed; no one knew anyone who had died. But a lot of people might have, sleeping through that long hot summer in air-tight rooms to keep safe from a bug that never existed except in somebody's mind

TRAINS, AN AVENUE TO ADVENTURE!

Since besides horse and buggy, trains were our only means of transportation, they played a big part in my life. Whenever I think of that little old brick Illinois Central Railroad station that still stands in my home town, memories start bubbling up out of my heart. It was from there I went to visit grandparents, aunts, uncles, friends, in Fort Dodge, Minneapolis, Cherokee, and, oh, my! Way out to Spokane Falls, as Spokane Washington was originally called. When I was eleven, I traveled to boarding school by train. Train fare was 2 cents a mile in those days.

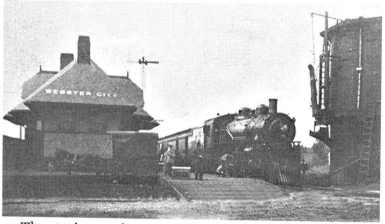

The train station was divided into three parts, a ladies' waiting room, a waiting room for men, and a ticket office, from where the constant click, click, clickety click of telegraph keys struck your ears the moment you stepped into the shabby, dusty-smelling building.

Naturally, rules in the station weren't rigid. Men were allowed on the woman's side. A lad spending those last few moments with his departing sweetheart; a husband helping his wife with babies, bundles, and baggage. But what woman wanted to venture onto the men's side and subject herself to the thick smoke of cigars, or the danger of stumbling over one of those obnoxious spittoons that were found in almost any male sitting room of that day? Certainly no "No Smoking" signs could be found in the women's area, for even the thought of his wife smoking would have turned a husband's hair grey!

In the middle of each room in winter stood a large pot-bellied stove, once possibly a shiny black but turned rusty brown by its many firings. People coming in from the cold, wrapped as for the arctic zone, stamping off snow, hurried to hold their hands to that welcoming warmth. In summer the room was suffocatingly hot, not even the whirr of an electric fan to stir the stagnant air.

A wide, well-worn, wooden platform ran in front of the station, extending far beyond it at each end. In frosty winter weather, except for trainmen and those who had good reason for being there, the platform was empty of people. In summer, folks walked back and forth, perched on a pile of trunks, or swung their feet from the baggage truck, smoking, gabbing, peering impatiently in the direction from which the train would come. Children, freed from Mother's hand, raced back and forth, screamed, played tag, heeding not at all their mothers' occasional warning, "Be careful that you don't fall off onto the tracks."

What an exciting place that station was in my childhood! Anything could happen there. Trains coming and going all day long. Our hotel "bus" meeting every one, taking passengers to the station, bringing others to the hotel.

Occasionally, if I had nothing better to do, I'd ride along, sitting up front with Joe, who sometimes would let me drive the horses. In cold or rainy weather I'd sit inside, but those drummers were a sober lot. Exchanging an occasional word or two, usually sitting glumly, staring straight ahead, jiggling with the movement of the bus, their minds possibly intent upon orders they hoped to get. When we arrived at the hotel, Joe would unload them, and, after they had registered, take them to their rooms. Now and then he might glean a dime or so from his service, but since tipping was not considered necessary, he'd more often get a mere "Thank you." "I've got a whole trunkfull of those," he often said!

Trains were the only practical means of transportation to places of any distance. I took my first rides when I was still a babe in arms, but the first rides I remember were to my grandparents' hotel in Fort Dodge twenty miles away. My father would put me on the train in care of the conductor whom he knew well. Grandfather would

---

RAIL-ROAD TIME-TABLES.

CHICAGO & NORTH-WESTERN.

SOUTH & EAST...
No. 10, Des Moines Passenger ...... 8:58 a m
No. 8, Chicago Passenger............ 3:45 p m
No. 16, Chicago Passenger.... .. 10:17 p m
No. 22, Way Freight,... ....9:15 a m

NORTH & WEST
No. 25, Dakota Express. ....5:50 a m
No. 7, Iowa Passenger.. .... 11:59 a m
No. 9, Des Moines Passenger.. .. .7:35 p m
No. 29, Des Moines Freight... ....3:05 p m
No. 21, Way Freight. .... 3:20 p m
No. 23, Freight. ....8:25 p m
Nos. 16 and 25 run daily. All other trains run daily except Sunday. Sunday

ILLINOIS CENTRAL.

GOING EAST
No. 2, Passenger Daily.. 12:13 a. m
No. 4, Passenger " ....11:50 a. m
No. 6, Passenger " ... 4:13 p. m
No. 60, Freight, " Stock ex Sat 8:51 a. m.
No. 82, Freight, " Way " Sund 10:00 a. m.

GOING WEST.
No. 1, Passenger Daily ....3:48 a. m
No. 3, Passenger " .... .. 6:00 p. m.
No. 5, Passenger " .... 12:40 p. m,
No. 51, Freight " Way, ex Sun, 1:57 p. m,
No. 53, Freight " .... 1:50 p. m.
No's 1 and 2 are solid vestibuled trains, carrying chair car and other modern improvements. Train No. 5 carries passengers to Fort Dodge. No. 60 carries passengers, Webster City to Waterloo and intermediate points. No's 93 and 94 carry passengers to and from all points on Waterloo section.
W. C. JOHNSTON, Agent.

CROOKED CREEK R. R. & COAL CO.
No. 2 leaves Webster City daily at 8:30 a. m.
Returning at 4:45 p. m.
No. 1 leaves Lehigh daily at 8:30 p. m.
Returning at 9:50 a. m.
Connections made at Webster City with trains going North, South, East or West.
F. E. WILLSON, Gen'l Pkr Agent.

IOWA CENTRAL.
Time of trains carrying passengers at Ackley, Iowa, effective July 1, 1901.

GOING NORTH.
No. 5, Twin City Limited, daily,.. ..2:12 a m
No. 1, St. Paul Mail, daily .... 11:17 a m
No. 3, Mason City Mail. ex. Sunday.. 7:14 p m
No. 9, Way Freight, ex. Sunday .....11:40 a m

GOING SOUTH.
No. 4, Peoria Mail, ex. Sunday.... .. 7:33 a m
No. 2, St. L. & K. C. Mail, daily...... 4:27 p m
No. 6, Peoria Limited. daily.. .. .... 1:46 a m
No. 10, Way Freight, ex. Sunday ....12:35 a m
No. 90, Through Freight, daily ......10:30 a m
Coupon tickets on sale to all points in the United States, Canada and Mexico. For rates, folders, etc., call on or address:
E. A. KOLAR, Agent, Ackley, Iowa.
A. B. CUTTS, Gen. Pass. and Ticket Agent, Minneapolis, Minn.

B. C. R. & N.—Time Table at Iowa Falls.
Going North.
Passenger, 601 B ....12:30 p m
" 605 A .... 3:38 a m
Passenger, 701 B................ .....12:40 p m
Freight, 643 B .... 7:00 a m
" 697 A .... 7:15 p m
" 741 B... ... ... 6:30 a m
Going South.
Passenger, 602 B .... 4:15 p m
" 608 A .... 9:55 p m
" 706 B arr .... 10:00 p m
Freight, 642 B .... 7:00 a m
" 692 A .... 11:00 a m
" 696 A .... 1:15 p m
A, daily. B, daily except Sunday.

---

meet me at the other end. When I came home it was a repeat performance, reversed. Hot, dirty, slow, as I look back, the gilded chariot or the flying carpet of fairyland were no more magic to my childish heart than those trains that took me to wherever I wanted to go.

On hot, summer days, to keep from suffocating, train windows were left open, allowing soot and smoke free access so that by the time one left the train she felt like a chimney sweep who hadn't had time to wash up. But to a child those open windows allowed an opportunity to stick a hand, or even a head, out and to feel the cooling wind rush past; or a try at touching the telephone poles as they went flying by. To a child those trains with their lights swinging from the ceiling, the dusty red plush seats, the worn red carpet running down the aisle were almost palatial. Happy when we could ride in one!

In those days I doubt the word sanitation was even in the dictionary. At the water coolers which stood at the end of each car there were no dainty paper cups to be discarded after using. Instead, dangling from a long chain hung a tin cup, often rusty, from which everyone, sick or well, drank. No wonder consumption, as TB was then called, ran rampant in the land. Not only was this convenient tin cup available on trains, but at any public drinking place as well.

No such things as litter laws, either. Matches, cigar stubs, candy wrappers, every unwanted article landed on the floor. Since chewing tobacco was a common habit then, when one had to expectorate, if no spittoon was handy, horrible as it may seem, it landed on the floor.

I once had an unhappy experience with this. On the way to my grandparents, alone, I was all dolled up in a pretty flowered summer dress, a big floppy hat atop my curls. But the part of my attire of which I was most proud was a pair of lacy white mitts that came almost up to my elbow.

Mitts were gloves that covered the hands but left the fingers bare. Because I was so proud of mine, I had my arms laid along on the arm of my seat so everyone could see them. An unfortunate mistake that was! For suddenly the car door opened and three soldiers, laughing noisily, perhaps a bit tipsy, entered the car, and just as they passed my seat one of them expectorated.[35]

Instead of landing on the floor, that ugly brown mess landed on my beautiful lacy mitt. Instantly apologetic, all contrition, the gentleman – or should I call him that? – whipped out his handkerchief and tried to wipe away the damage. Nothing, however, could eradicate that ugly brown stain nor the dismay in my young heart. Crushed, no longer did I lay my arm out for admiration. Blinded by tears, I stripped off my mitts and stuffed them in my little purse.

A bête noire[33] of those days were the tunnels through which trains occasionally had to bore their way. We were always warned of their approach by the brakeman's coming through the car lighting the oil lamps swinging from the ceiling with his smoking torch, so we wouldn't be in the dark. Still, those tunnels always frightened me.

"Just sit quiet," my mother would say, "We'll soon be through it." And once we were, the world seemed brighter than it had before we entered the tunnel. Somehow I've carried that thought into my adult life.

When confronted by troubles that seem too black to handle, Mother's words come back to me: "Just sit quiet. We'll soon be through it." And, oddly, once my black mood has evaporated, my world does look brighter that it did before, and I seem competent to handle any problem.

Sometimes we'd go to visit aunts, uncles, cousins in Minneapolis, which we kids liked because it was a longer trip than the one we made to Fort Dodge to visit our grandparents. One incident shows how leisurely life was in those days. There was a certain spot between my home and Minneapolis where the train would stop—way out in the country—and allow a boy to board the train with a basket of large white water-lilies to sell to the passengers.

But the best trip of all was the one when Mother took me, my younger brother, and my two-year old sister to Spokane Falls to visit my mother's sister, Aunt Louise[36] and family, and her mother, Grandmother Mundt, who lived with them.

I've often thought that Mother was rather brave to 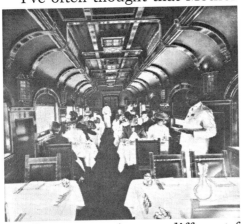 take such small children on so long a trip that involved eating and sleeping on a train. But it was sleeping in those curtained berths, eating in the dining car, being waited on by a jolly Negro waiter, so different from the hotel dining room, that delighted me most. We spent seven whole days on that train!

Although we had both lower and upper berths, Mother's fear that we might fall out had all four of us sleeping huddled together in the lower berth, while we kept our clothes in the upper. It must have been difficult dressing three lively children in so small a space, but she didn't want to go trailing with us down to the wash room.

How she kept our clothes from becoming wrinkled I'll never know. Especially since to me, never particular about how I handled things, was relegated

the job of putting the clothes overhead. It was difficult doing this, while trying to keep hidden behind the curtains. One morning when I was getting our clothes down, my foot slipped, my hand lost its hold on the upper berth, and I went tumbling out into the aisle.

If you've never seen an embarrassed child, you should have seen me then! Every other berth had been made up. All the passengers had evidently breakfasted, and settled down for the day. They were reading, playing cards, talking with each other, while there I was, picking myself up, wearing only my long woolen nightgown. The speed with which I got back into that berth has never been equaled!

Our reason for sleeping so late that morning was a terrific storm we had had during the night. Thunder and lightening kept up an almost constant bombardment. Mother, who really was afraid of thunder storms, closed the curtains over the windows, but to me the storm was exciting. I kept peeking out and with every flash of lightening got terrifying glimpses of the wooded valley far below us. Mother, conscious of the sleeping passengers, kept quieting my sister who, with every sharp clap of thunder, would waken and start crying. It was well toward morning before we got to sleep.

That train was far superior to any I'd ever ridden on before.

Slick, polished, comfortable, efficient, it was beautiful. It ran on the track built by Jim Hill. That name is one I'd often heard while visiting my grand parents in their Minneapolis hotel. My grandfather was a great admirer of Hill, and our Sunday drives were often taken to show some visitor or friend Jim Hill's palatial home on a hill over-looking the city.

Grandfather had met Hill, but to hear him boast of

Jim Hill you might believe he was responsible for his accomplishments. He never tired of telling of them, and of his insatiable interest in anything pertaining to railroads. How, in an

144

emergency, Hill would get out and work with his men, as skilled with pick and shovel as the best of them. How he knew the names of his every superintendent and chief foreman, and could even call older men who had worked for him for a long time by their first names.

As a result, hard-pusher though he was, Jim Hill was a hero to those who worked for him. Grandfather told a story of a Swede who, exhorted in a prayer meeting, was asked, "Won't you come forward Ole, and work for Jesus?" "Naw," replied Ole with an unemotional shake of his head, "I got good job with Jim Hill."

So deeply was that name engrained into my mind by Grandfather's admiration for Hill, that now when I hear it, it's as if it were the name of someone I too knew personally.

The train trip to Spokane Falls was fun during the day. The train had to climb mountains, and sometimes when the pull was especially hard, there'd be an engine up front, pulling, and another behind, pushing. When we went around a hairpin sharp curve, we could see both the engine in front and the one behind. In some places the track ran so close to the edge of a mountain that we feared we might fall off. Sometimes we'd be walled in by trees, and once, going over a trestle, there seemed to be nothing between us and the dark boiling waters of a river far below.

To me, the whole trip was filled with fun and excitement from beginning to end. As I remember, we three children behaved very well. Eventually we reached Aunt Louise's, whose house was far out on the edge of town, almost in the country, and there we found new excitement. At one side of their house was a huge spruce forest in which we children used to play, and where I would gather spruce "gum" which my mother liked to chew.

But, most exciting was an Indian trail that ran through the forest, which the Indians used when going to town. The trail was beyond view of the house, but as I'd never seen an Indian I was always in hopes I would. It was a hope never realized. But a story told by my grandmother did almost as well. One day, when she was young, and in the house alone, a big, burly Indian, all decked out in paint and feather, came to the door and demanded, "Me want food."

Whether he used those exact words I don't know. If Grandmother was frightened, she didn't say, but one thing was for sure, she scurried around and saw that that Indian got the food he wanted! By the time Grandmother told me this story she was so old she'd forgotten most of the details, so I never learned whether the Indian ate the food in her kitchen, or carried it away with him.

One experience I had while we were at Aunt Louise's I'll never forget. We children were playing out of doors when, because of some altercation with cousin Adolph, he started chasing me, and I ran into the house, intending to escape through the front door, he close behind me. My getaway lay through a narrow space between two tables. Unfortunately for me, Aunt Louise had set a wonderful kettle of her vegetable soup on one table, handle sticking out, and as I ran, I hit the handle, knocking the kettle to the floor, the soup and me with it. Naturally my aunt, her dinner ruined, was furious, and once I was gotten out of the soup I got a good licking from my mother, a job that would have been relegated to my father had he been there.

Sobbing wildly, I ran into my grandmother's room and threw myself down on her bed. I hadn't escaped without being burned, and to ease the pain of my aching leg, I pulled a heavy pillow out of Grandmother's chair, laid it on top of the burn, hoping the pressure would help it, and sobbed myself to sleep.

When finally I awakened and called my mother to come and see my injured leg, she was stricken with contrition. For one side of my leg, from knee to ankle, was a huge and watery blister, puffed up at least an inch high. At my mother's cry of distress, the whole family rushed in and I've never seen people turn so quickly from condemnation to sympathy as they did when they saw my leg. Someone ran for salve, someone argued that tea was better for burns. Aunt Louise ran for an old sheet to tear into bandages.

I soon began to think that burn was well worth all the attention it brought me. All the time it was healing I was petted, loved, humored, aided, and abetted. Instead of being treated like a criminal, I was treated as a person highly wronged. I regretted when that bandage finally was needed no more, and I returned to being a normal child, treated as children usually are!

SECRET GIFTS OF FLOWERS!

May Basket Day! Hang your basket filled with flowers on a friend's door, ring the bell, and run! No one wanted to get caught in the act of delivering a May Basket; the secrecy of the ritual made May Day both exciting and fun.

Our preparations for May Day began well over a week before the big day. We'd begin by going around to our local department stores for pasteboard boxes to trim. My favorite containers were the round boxes delicate baby ribbon came on. By removing one end of the round box, one had a beautiful little receptacle, just perfect for trimming. But we'd take any small pasteboard boxes we could get, cutting them into whatever shape we wanted. Even the long boxes that spools of thread came in, although they were rather awkward, could be fashioned into May baskets. Almost any box, after it had been dressed up with tissue paper and wild flowers, made a good appearance.

We bought our tissue paper and crepe paper at the drug store. I preferred crepe because by pulling out the edges, a ruffled effect could be produced. The tissue and crepe paper came in big squares and hung on racks. I always had trouble deciding what colors to choose. Pastel colors were generally the best for May baskets, and I liked them because they were dainty.

With all our materials ready, Mother would set up a table in the living room, produce a bottle of white paste, blunt end scissors, and we'd go to work. Mother was always around to help us. The best thing was, she liked to do things like that; she was a mother who enjoyed working and playing with her children. She'd advise us how to paste the paper on the boxes, help us cut the paper up into strips to braid for handles, and show us how to make little bows out of baby ribbon. When we were all done, she'd set our baskets aside in a box, until we had gathered our wild flowers.

Flower picking was as much fun as making the baskets. For several years we had a wonderful Sunday school teacher who, just before May Day, would take us out to Hogs Back, a wooded hill on the edge of town where every kind of wild flower imaginable grew: Anemones, bluebells, violets, and my favorite – Dutchman's Britches. Though the distance from town to the hill was a good mile or more, we always walked, trudging along in the hot Iowa sun. At least half of that distance was along railroad track, and we'd see who could cover the most ties with one giant step, vying with each other as to who could walk the farthest along the rail without falling off.

And how cool the woods, how soft the grass when finally we reached our destination! Flowers grew everywhere, but we were by then so hungry and thirsty that without picking a flower, we'd sit down and eat our sandwiches and drink our lemonade. Revived, we'd jump up and start picking flowers. No use trying to get ahead of the next fellow; there was enough for everyone. We generally headed home with our baskets loaded.

Halfway to town, at the side of the road, was a long, moss-lined watering trough into which an artesian well poured the most delicious water. The water gushed out of an old, rusty, iron pipe. Some of us would climb up on an old stone beside the tank, put our mouths against the cold iron, and drink the water, just as it came from the pipe. Others would drink from an old tin can that hung on a stake beside the trough. Germs? Had anyone mentioned them we'd only have laughed. We'd never even heard of such things. And even if we had, we'd still scoff: "Believe in bugs we can't see? Impossible!"

Flushed and hot, our hair wet with perspiration and stringing down around our faces, it seemed we couldn't get enough of that water! Our teacher would keep admonishing us, "Don't drink too much girls. It's not good to drink so much water when you're so hot." But we needed that water to give us strength and stamina for the distance yet to travel.

Once home, we put our already wilting wildflowers into water to freshen for the next day's baskets. And how beautiful and dainty those baskets looked, filled to overflowing with the flowers we'd had such fun gathering. But more fun was still to come! Just after dusk, we'd go from the home of one friend to another, hanging a May basket on a door knob, or setting it on a porch floor. Then we'd ring the bell, dash for the nearest bush – for the back of the house – anywhere not to be caught. After we'd finished our clandestine deliveries, we'd go home, empty-handed, and find a whole bunch of May Baskets waiting for us!

SCENES OF SUMMER FUN!

I loved the summers I spent with my grandparents in Minneapolis and Lake Minnetonka. Especially when they ran the hotel on the corner of Nicollet Avenue, the Windsor.[37]

I remember watching the lamplighters at dusk, and running in fear from the chimney sweeps.

For it was there, instead of having to share a room with my sisters, as I did at home, I had a room all to myself, to use as I pleased. After my Grandmother tucked me into bed at night and turned out the light, I'd wait a while, then turn the light back on and read. One summer I read Grimm's and Anderson's fairy tales, Hawthorne's Tanglewood Tales, and any mythology I could get my hands on. I'd read until I could no longer hold my eyes open, then tuck my book under my pillow and go to sleep.

I'd often be wakened early by the sound of rumbling wagon wheels and horses hooves striking against cobblestones, so I'd get up and watch the men and their wagons on their way to work, enjoying the sounds of the awakening city. Then maybe I'd crawl back into bed and read some more, or go back to sleep until Grandmother called me for breakfast. I was given responsibility there too.

Often Grandmother, who sewed a lot, would send me to the Glass Block, as Donaldson's[38] Department store was then called, for thread to match the sample she gave me; or with a note to the clerk for another yard of goods like some she'd gotten a day or two before. The store was but a short distance from the hotel, and with only horse-drawn vehicles, there was small danger of being run over.

The Bijou Theater, too, was only a short distance away. As at my father's hotel, the leading actors

generally stayed at the Windsor, and we received complimentary play tickets. I never missed a matinee and was allowed to go alone, which made me feel very important. Although I saw mostly the same melodramas I had seen at the theater at home, I enjoyed going to the shows nevertheless.

I remember a scene from one of the plays vividly: the villain laying a small child on the slowly moving belt of a sawmill, the belt carrying the child toward the whirling saw and certain death, until, just at the last possible moment, the hero rushed in and grabbed the child and carried her to safety. How I sat there, gripped in terror, not even breathing, until that girl was rescued! I resolved then that I would be a playwright when I grew up, and write even better plays than those I saw and enjoyed.

Another thing I greatly enjoyed in Minneapolis was the Salvation Army group that met each evening at the corner by the hotel. Music by a drummer, a horn-player, a tambourine played by a pretty lass in an attractive uniform and fetching bonnet soon drew a crowd. After the group had sung, prayed, and a man had preached, invoking men to turn to their Maker, the lass moved among the crowd holding out her tambourine for donations. Unfortunately, that move dispersed the crowd quickly!

But I, watching from the parlor window just above them was so impressed by all this that I confided to my grandmother that I wanted to be a Salvation Army girl when I grew up, and wondered if my father would let me. She was sure he wouldn't, but soothed me by suggesting that by the time I grew up I'd probably want to be something else. How right she was!

One morning, the usual humdrum of the hotel was broken by a frantic call from Aunt Grace,[39] my grandparents' daughter who also lived in Minneapolis. Elmer, their four year old son, was lost. They'd looked everywhere, but were unable to find him. Scarcely had Grandfather hung up the receiver, than he had Grandmother and me in the backseat of the surrey, and he was racing his black team toward Aunt Grace's.

Alas! We were stopped by a funeral procession. Grandfather reigned the horses impatiently, until seeing a break in the line, he dashed through. Instantly Grandmother was berating him. What a stupid thing to do! Didn't he know that to break through a funeral procession was bad luck? Now they would never find Elmer!

It looked as if she were right. Up one street, down another, with a weeping Aunt Grace beside

Grandmother. She explained how one moment Elmer

had been playing on the apartment house stairs, and that the next time they'd looked out, he was gone. "He couldn't have disappeared so quickly," Aunt Grace sobbed, "Someone must have kidnapped him!"

But when we checked back home, there was Elmer, playing contentedly with his blocks. A neighbor had found him, wandering a few blocks away, crying because he was lost, and brought him home.

So, at least one of Grandmother's superstitions was invalidated! She had plenty in reserve, however. It was a popular time for superstitions. People feared black cats crossing their path, walking under ladders, opening umbrellas in the house, and the seven years bad luck brought about by breaking a mirror. Grandmother predicted so much bad luck that it seemed one could scarcely move without bringing a curse upon themselves!

Sometimes, when visiting my grandparents in Minneapolis, I'd go spend a week or so with Aunt Teenie,[40] my mother's sister. Although plump instead of slim, with her dark hair and soft brown eyes, she was much like my mother – kind and warm. She kept her youngest son, Herman, in kilts and corkscrew curls until he was quite a large boy. I liked to stand beside her, watching her wind those curls around her finger, smoothing them with a brush. I still think it remarkable how patiently Herman endured this ordeal.

My cousin Charlie was more my age and we had a unique way of entertaining ourselves. Uncle Carl[41] was a stone cutter in a tombstone shop. He'd bring home the sand-like dust (floor sweepings, really) that resulted from the stone cutting. Charlie and I would spend hours filling bottles with these different colored "sands", seeing who could get the prettiest patterns. Sometimes neighborhood kids would work with us, too, but we wouldn't let them take their bottles home!

The first time I ever tasted blueberries, for which I developed a life-long love, was at Aunt Teenie's. She'd often have a big glass bowl of them on the table that we'd eat with sugar and milk for desert. It was a treat I never had in Iowa, as blueberries didn't grow there.

When at Aunt Teenie's we always went at least once on a picnic to Minnehaha Falls. In fact, Minnehaha was so much a part of my childhood that I still feel as if I own a share in it. The Falls were then way out beyond the edge of town. As no such thing as a hot dog or hamburger stand  existed, Aunt Teenie would pack a big basket lunch and we'd go out on the street car. The round trip cost a nickel, with a free transfer ticket if you had to change from one car to another. I loved the summer street cars, open on the sides, seats facing front. The wind blowing against my face, the clang-clang of the bell, was half the enjoyment.

Minnehaha was all woods, with an abundant flow of water rushing over the rocks, splashing into the brook below. Before my time there had been a railed walk behind the Falls, where one could enjoy the scene from behind the water, but the rocks had eventually so disintegrated that the walk had to be abandoned.

I often went with my Grandparents out to the Falls, too, but this was with horse and buggy, a Sunday drive just for a look.

As there were no other children to romp and play with, this didn't thrill me much.

I spent a few summers at Lake Minnetonka where, along with the Windsor Hotel, my grandparents were managing a large and impressive summer hotel – the Minnetonka House.[42] Certainly the clientele were

158

entirely different from those of the Windsor Hotel. Gleaming open carriages drawn by spirited horses would drive up to the entrance and discharge expensively gowned, often pompous matrons. Wearing long skirts, big of bust and hips, with tiny waists, and big hats; while the porter unloaded their luggage, the ladies would daintily lift their skirts and ascend the long flight of steps that led to the wide porch and disappear into the office.

Sometimes men would be with them; important looking men impeccably dressed, wearing high hats, and often sporting grey spats over their shiny, pointed, patent leather shoes.

Or sometimes it would be a young mother and father, with a bevy of children who, regardless of parental admonitions, would race up the stairs into  the office ahead of their parents. It was these children who interested me. I, standing on the sidelines, would watch as they passed me by, wondering which ones would be nice to play with.

As there were generally plenty of children around, it was a gay summer. We had parties, played games on the beach, swam, and went rowing.

As usual, where there are children there is generally a bully or mischief maker and we had ours! One day he pushed me into the canna-bordered fountain in front of the hotel, from which I emerged, dripping wet, my hair stringing down into my eyes.

Once he altered the bulletin board in the hall announcing, "Whist party held in the drawing room at eight thirty," by changing the "d" on held to a second "l".

There were many titters before that "error" was corrected! But at his birthday party he had the most delicious cake, and I've never forgotten it. Ice cream cake it was called; purest white, thickly frosted, made by the hotel chef, it was  the finest-textured, moistest cake I've ever eaten.

I used to wonder if older people had fun at the lake. Trussed-up dowagers, they'd sit in the comfortable rockers on the wide porch that faced the water,  knitting, crocheting, gossiping, nodding over a book they were reading. Tame stuff! Men might be there too, in little groups, hashing over news or politics, but never interesting me enough to listen.

We children had a great time playing in the water at the edge of the lake. Splashing each other, throwing beach balls, or sitting around building sand castles kept us busy and out of our elders' way. The bathing suits we girls wore were comical. Made of wool, high-necked, with elbow length sleeves, and a skirt over ruffled knee-length bloomers, we also wore stockings and light weight slippers, held on by narrow ribbons laced around our legs. A ruffled bathing cap left only our faces and forearms uncovered! Yet, in spite of our restricting clothing, we

did our share of squirming, jumping about, and, sometime, even actually swimming!

One summer a cousin and I made an occupation out of catching frogs. We'd scramble through the reeds at the edge of the lake after our prey, which we'd sell to the eating houses along the lake that served fried frogs legs. We never got rich at this occupation, but it gave

us enough money to take an occasional ride on the pleasure boat, the Tonka, around the lake. It was really about the only thing we could spend money on at the lake.

I liked our trips into Minneapolis, behind Grandfather's speedy horses, to see how things were doing there. Grandmother complained of the dust kicked up by the horses' hooves, but I loved the ride, especially because of the sumac I saw growing along the way with its big red spikes. This was the first sumac I'd ever seen; it didn't grow in Iowa. My love for green and growing things began at the lake. At home, the small space in front of the hotel where grass might have grown was covered with gravel. The only green things were in the back-yard where I played. I remember big clumps of Burdock from which my sister and I would stick the burrs together to make dishes – plates, boxes, baskets, cups – then we'd play with them in my playhouse. It's remarkable what things we children did, at home and at the lake, when we were left to our own devices!

THE FABULOUS FOURTH!

In my childhood, the fourth of July ranked second only to circuses in terms of excitement. A parade! The exhilarating music of a marching band! Both sides of Main street lined with horse-drawn vehicles, the wide walks crowded with people all in holiday attire. Farmers, both local and from surrounding towns, laying work aside for one day, driving into town to celebrate!

The hotel porch crowded with sightseers, the dining room filled to overflowing, everyone rushing around to keep everyone fed and happy, and the air filled with the sound of smoke and exploding firecrackers. I, doing my share of the celebrating, had saved up pennies for weeks to get my supply of sparklers, pinwheels, torpedoes, and firecrackers. They came in bunches all laced together, and I pulled them out one by one, lit them, and tossed them out of my hands, quick! Then I stood back and watched the older kids ignite and throw the bigger, louder, firecrackers. A little envious, but proud to have made my share of the clamor, I remembered happily the other fireworks I still had stored away to light later in the evening.

How hard it was for me to get to sleep the night before the big day! Then, scarcely had I closed my eyes, it seemed, than even before daylight the sharp bang of a giant firecracker awakened me; then another, and another, until they popped all around me like popcorn in a popper. Impatiently, I'd wait for daylight and then crawl out of bed, into my clothes, and start in on my own celebration.

My favorite Fourth of Julys were the ones when my parents' friends had a picnic over at Charlie Soule's home. The Soules lived over the tracks (the right side of the tracks!), where some of the earlier settlers had built lovely homes that to my childish eyes appeared to be mansions. This part of town was near the river[43] and was naturally wooded. Lovely big oaks, I remember us kids gathering the acorns.

The Soule and Allington homes took up an entire block. I liked the Allington home best. It was pink with a wide porch encircling the front and one side of the house, and a large, curved plate glass window overlooking the street. The room I liked best in that house was the conservatory, or green house, located off the dining room. A mass of greenery, it had many exotic plants I'd never seen before, and was filled with the fragrance of moist earth and flowers.

"When I grow up and get married, Mrs. Allington," I told her one day, "I'm going to have a room in my house just like this!"

She laughed, a soft, amused laugh. "I hope you can, Irene," she said, "but that's still a long way off."

Mrs. Allington was one of my mother's best friends, and one of those I liked best. Small and plump, with dark hair and merry brown eyes, always dressed in fluffy, ruffled bright-colored dresses, she was effusive

164

and warm-hearted. I liked Mr. Allington too. A big tall man like my father, he was sort of gangling and awkward, but always jolly. As owner of both the town bottling works and a furniture store, he was a big name in the town.

The reason I liked to go to their house was to play with their son, Guy, who was about my age. We always played at his house so we wouldn't be bothered by my brother and sisters! Although the Allington's lived a goodly distance from the hotel, I was allowed to walk to their home, but never without being cautioned, "Watch out for trains." There were several tracks to cross, on which trains were always puffing, or backing, or side-tracking, as trains ran through our town all hours of the day.

The Soule home, painted brown, was dark and gloomy, inside and out. And Mrs. Soule was as different from Guy's mother, as a drab moth is different from a gay butterfly. I never saw her in anything but a plain, dark dress. Though she was a kind and pleasant woman, she was reserved and somewhat aloof. As I grew older, I learned she was one of the first Christian Scientists in our town, at a time when that religion was far from being accepted, and very religious.

Charlie Soule was just as friendly and outgoing as his wife was withdrawn. As manager and stockholder in the tile factory, he was an important person, and well liked by everyone who knew him.

The Soule's one daughter, Maude, a large, auburn-haired girl, built like her mother but with the disposition of her father, was witty and fun-loving. She had a beautiful voice, and she generally sang in church, or at any town celebration.

Another reason I liked to have our Fourth of July parties at the Soule's home was because they had a music box, the only one in town. So big that it came almost up to my chin, it played steel "records," about two feet across, they resembled the circular blades of a buzz saw, so heavy that they could be changed only by an adult. The machine had to be wound by hand, and this was such a fascinating job that we kids were always vying with one another as to who could get the job!

The most exciting spot in the Soule home was a long room in the cellar. Along each side of the room was a long table with enough fireworks to last an ordinary family a month or two. Mr. Soule hadn't forgotten us children either; there was a goodly supply of small firecrackers, sparklers, and torpedoes that we began shooting off the moment we arrived.

Once, however, I got out of line. Wanting to see for myself what that cellar contained, I wandered down there on my own, a stick of lighted punk in my hand. I doubt if any child was ever hustled out of a place so fast as I was when the men working there saw that piece of lighted punk I carried!

"Don't you know, kid," they shouted as they fairly flung me out of the room, "that if you set off even one thing with that punk, it would set off everything, and the whole house might go up in smoke?" If I didn't know that fact before, I sure learned it then!

The Fourth of July dinner at a long table set on the well-shaded lawn between the Soule and Allington home, temporarily  interrupted our interest in fireworks. The table was covered with a long linen cloth, linen napkins, china

166

dishes, and silver tableware. The effect of gleaming china, silver and white linen, set against the cool green colors of the grass and trees was breathtaking. And what a feast was spread out on that table! We gorged ourselves with wild abandon, not one soul caring a single bit about the extra pounds that rich food might put on his figure!

The climax of the holiday came at night with the shooting off of the Roman candles, sky rockets, and bombs that went hurtling toward the heavens, finally bursting into a shower of brilliantly colored sparks that rained down toward the earth. It was well toward midnight before the supply of fireworks was exhausted and another Fourth of July ended. Now all that was

left was for weary parents to gather up their sleepy children, pack them into buggies, drive them home, and tumble them into bed.

THE DAY THE CIRCUS CAME TO TOWN

The arrival of the circus in our small town was an event long awaited.[44] The advertising men arrived first, and plastered immense posters on every available billboard in town. Junie and I would survey the wonders those posters depicted with awe. The man on the flying trapeze! Beautiful women, hanging only by their teeth, circling round and round high up at the top of the tent! Diminutive ladies in flouncy skirts dancing upon the back of prancing horses. Performing elephants! Lions and tigers, growling viciously, but obeying the man with the whip.

Immediately we began saving our money for the big day! Junie and I were certain that we'd want more money for ice cream, popcorn, lemonade, and peanuts than our parents would be willing to give us!

I can't remember a time when I didn't love circuses. I imagine I attended my first one as a babe in arms – the arms of my fun-loving Grandfather. He would never have missed the chance of taking his first grandchild to such a spectacular event. He doubtless carried me all around the animal tent, trying to explain to me the mysteries of each animal.

Of this I have no memories, but I would wager that it happened. For later I remember how I used to move from cage to cage holding Grandfather's hand, both awed and frightened by the lions, tigers, and bears, pacing back and forth, confined to the limited space of their cages; wild animals that had once roamed freely over unlimited acres! Camels, giraffes, elephants! How I cringed when the hippopotamus lifted his gaping mouth out of the water, looking as if he wanted to swallow me.

The glass cage with the writhing snakes! Once I was watching as a beautiful lady wrapped an ugly snake around her slim, sequined body, when my grandfather, so that I might see better, lifted me up onto a box sitting beside the cage. Was that ever a mistake! I broke right through the top of the box and out jumped a dozen rabbits, scattering in all directions. Instantly, circus hands appeared from nowhere to go dashing after them.

We didn't stay around to see what happened next; we got out of there quick! The poor rabbits! We later learned they were food for the snakes, and I was glad they escaped.

Grandfather then bought me a glass of lemonade, and peanuts to feed the elephants. I was frightened as that pink-lined snout reached out for the morsel in my hand, and I dropped the peanut. But those mammoth animals with the constant fanning of their huge hears, the restless swaying of their trunks, fascinated me, and once I learned they wanted only the peanut I offered them, (not me too!) I enjoyed feeding them.[45]

One of the most exciting events of circus day was the unloading of the circus train. One of my early joys was to tumble sleepily out of bed in the small hours of the morning to walk the several blocks to the tracks to watch the circus train roll into town.

Sometimes my mother would go with me, often pushing a baby carriage, enjoying the excitement almost as much as I did! As I grew older, Junie went with me, after having spent the night at the hotel, so we could get up and go off together.

Often when we arrived at the station, half the town was already there, milling around, sitting on the edge of the freight house platform, swinging their feet, for almost always the train was late. Then suddenly someone would cry, "Here she comes" and we'd all jump to attention, hearing the faint, far-away toot of a whistle, seeing a thin spiral of smoke against the sky. Then the train would be right before our eyes, puffing into the station, squirting steam, as it pulled to a slow stop.

Immediately all was a scene of bustling activity. Wagons carrying tents, tent poles, and seats, were rolled off the first flat cars. Then came the canvas covered wagons, under whose flapping canvases we knew were elaborately decorated cages carrying wild animals of all sorts – lions, tigers, bears! Elephants lumbering down the ramps were immediately put to

work pulling wagons, shifting them about, seeming instinctively to know what to do. Beautiful prancing horses were led out of box cars. Lions roaring, seals barking, horses neighing, elephants trumpeting, --such strange noises for our usually quiet mid-western town! Men hurrying in all directions, barking out orders. But there was order in all the confusion; everyone knew just what to do and did it. Giving no heed to us curious onlookers, unless we got in their way – and then we were firmly ordered aside.

Finally, distracting our attention, young, pretty girls, in small groups came strolling by. In their long dark dresses, they bore little resemblance to the fairy creature who later, in dazzling attire, would perform such acts of daring on trapeze, highwire, or horseback that spectators, on the edge of their seats, hardly dared to breath until the act ended! Now, walking slowly on their way to the circus grounds, talking and laughing, they completely ignored those of us who stared at them. Junie and I gazed after those girls enviously; thinking of what glamorous lives they led, we half-decided that when we grew up we'd be circus girls too!

To get to the circus grounds, the performers, like the rest of us, had to walk a good two miles or more.

 We'd wonder, Junie and I, as we straggled along after them, how they could make it in time for the parade. For once the last wagon had left the freight yard, the crowd set out for the circus grounds.

Once there, what a conglomeration of giddy sights; everywhere, something happening! The big top lying flat in the ground! Men, with huge mallets, pounding tent stakes into the dirt. Small boys running in every direction, carrying water to the elephants, doing any job, big or little, that would get them a free ticket to the show.

A dainty little lady, balancing herself with a ruffled parasol, walked a tight wire high in the air. A stand selling pink lemonade, where we stopped to quench our thirsts and bought popcorn to quiet the grumbling of our hungry stomachs. A crowd gathered around a table where a young squirt, straw hat on the side of his head, was moving three walnut shells about, playing what our parents called the "shell game."

The smell of food led us to the dining tent, open on all sides, where circus people, at long tables, sat eating breakfast. But the tent "next door" looked more fascinating. The sides were rolled up so that we saw people moving about inside, unpacking trunks, presumably getting ready for the parade.

But it was the people outside the tent who held our attention. A man, shirtless, suspenders hanging at his side, shaving before a small mirror fastened to a tent pole; a woman washing her blond hair; another hanging up garments she had just washed. In a canvas chair, a pretty girl sat sewing spangles on a slinky looking garment. Talking, laughing, as they worked at common-place duties, similar to those our mothers did at home. We stood gaping, listening, getting all bubbly inside if one of them spoke to us, asking our name, and how old we were. How we would brag to our friends that we actually talked with some of the circus people!

I remember it all so well; the heat of the sun, the smell of trampled grass, the earth torn by heavy wagon wheels, the unmistakable odor of animals. Standing goggle-eyed, we watched them stretch into place the long banner in front of the freak tent: the sword swallower, the midgets, the fat lady, the living skeleton, the wild man of Borneo gnawing at the hunk of raw meat they'd thrown in his cage. The sea of tents, glistening white in the blazing sun. Such are my memories of the marvels of a circus grounds before the show opened.

But the wonders of the day had only just begun! Back at the hotel we found a crowd already gathering on the porch to watch the parade. The side street lined with horse-drawn vehicles, the sidewalks beginning to fill; here and there on rooftops, or in open windows, people waited.

We kids and Mother had a special seat on a balcony hanging outside one of the hotels' third story windows. From there we could see clear to the end of Main Street, down which the parade would come.

We waited impatiently, Mother striving to keep order, pulling us back as we leaned too far over the balustrade. Finally, at the first faint strains of band

music, we became still. Far down the street, we saw a man on horseback, carrying a banner. Soon he passed by beneath us, with a squadron of beautiful gowned girls on high-stepping horses following behind him! Next came the band wagon, gold and glittering, atop it the band playing intoxicating tunes that have no equal.

Then the gaudily decorated cages, opened now, and displaying tigers, lions, bears, and frolicking monkeys. We'd laugh at the clowns tumbling on and off donkeys, and at the man on stilts, who with his high hat nearly reached the tops of buildings. At last! The man on the prancing horse, riding up and down both sides of the street, crying out in his deep sotto voice, "Hold your horses, everybody. The elephants are coming!"

"Why are horses afraid of elephants, Mama?" we'd ask. She never had an answer. The horses paid no attention to the camels, the giraffes, the zebras,  but as the elephants came shuffling along, they'd rear up, toss back their heads, and let out terror-stricken screams.

At the first faint sound of the calliope my heart would sink, knowing the end of the parade was approaching. But Mother smiled; she loved the calliope. She watched as it came up the street, as it passed below us, and followed it with her eyes as it moved out of sight. So we'd crawl back through the window, and go down to lunch.

After we ate, Mother would take us to the circus. She would spend most of her time there digging into her purse, buying us peanuts, popcorn,  lemonade, and balloons. We liked best to go with her alone, without Father who always put a damper on spending. Never would he buy tickets to the after show, nor outside the tent, the side shows as Mother would. The secret? She was as curious as the kids and believed in the whole works!

Once the extravaganza ended, Junie and I would hurry home to practice all the tricks that might one day make us circus girls. Lacking a trapeze, we'd hang from the footboard of the bed by our knees, turn somersaults forward, backwards; trying to do a split, marveling that what "they" did so easily we couldn't do at all. With the wall as a prop we could almost stand on our heads!

But my last taste of the circus was not yet over. Lying in bed in the dark, I'd listen to the rumble of wagons as they passed my window on their way back to the train. Or, if not too sleepy, I'd get out of bed and go to the window to watch the dim silhouettes of

horses, camels, and elephants plodding wearily to their "beds", to be ready for the next day's performance. Then I'd creep wearily back into bed, reliving the wonder of the day until I fell asleep.

COUNTRY FAIR DAYS

No sky writers performed daring stunts above the gaping crowds of those long ago country fairs. No fearless pilots zoomed their flimsy planes up into the sky, sent them spiraling down to earth, only at the last moment pulling them into a series of rolls and somersaults to the wild excitement of the cheering onlookers below. Nor could the tiny figure of a man be seen walking along the edge of a tilted plane wing, standing on his head, hanging by his knees from a dangling trapeze.

No! This was before the days of barnstorming, in which even our hero, Lindbergh, played no part. Indeed, it was so long ago that planes hadn't even been considered, much less invented. Oh, well! Maybe the Wright brothers had a few bees buzzing around in their bonnets as to what might be, but who'd ever heard of them?

Nor were there any dare-devil, hell-drivers to astound grandstand audiences with their fantastic speed, their leaping off dead-end ramps, over gaping chasms; rolling, somersaulting, crashing their cars together, until cars finally burst into flames, and their drivers, unscathed and unscarred, stepped from their burning vehicles, smiling to receive the plaudits of their cheering admirers.

No! This was back in the nineties when horse-drawn vehicles were the main means of transportation, and gas propelled vehicles not even thought of. No planes, no cars, at those early country fairs. So what was there for excitement? People needed more than cattle, hogs, horses, and sheep for a drawing card. Women needed more that the products of the exhibition hall – baked or canned goods, fancy work, fruits, and vegetables to amuse or astound them.

Of course there were the free acts, the man who dove from a high tower into a tiny tub of water; the daring stunts of the man on the high tight wire. But the big  event of those early fairs was the inflation and ascension of the balloon. Should you arrive at the fair grounds early enough you would find the balloon nothing but a big blob of colorful material, lying lifeless on the ground. A small knot of onlookers may already have arrived to watch the beginning of the inflation. Two or three assistants might be there, following closely the orders of a small, agile man in a gaudy robe and tights, who seemed to be everywhere at once, barking out instructions.

Gradually, as the heat from the fire inside it increased, that big blob of lifeless material seemed to  come alive. It would begin to rise, to bubble up, to swell, to sway. To the joy of the excited onlookers, it rose higher and higher, its wrinkles smoothed out, and it began to take shape.

I have no idea how long it took until the balloon was filled to its capacity. Only that when it was above the ground, a large basket dangling below it, that agile young man, master of ceremonies, tossed his robe aside, climbed bravely into the basket, and gave orders for the anchoring ropes to be cut. Then, as the balloon rose above the heads of the crowd, a roar of delight went up from the throats of the onlookers. Men waved their arms, tossed their hats up into the air. The balloon rose higher and higher; the wind caught it, and carried it off in an oblique direction. Not until it was little more than a speck against the blue of the sky, did the crowd disperse.

But interest didn't wane. Speculations were made, bets placed, as to where the balloon would land. In a tree? In the jungle or a swamp? In a river or lake? Or, by some happy fluke, in the middle of a large clear meadow?

Once the balloon was on its way, those who wanted to be sure where it landed, took off in horse and buggy, hopefully in the right direction, to be in on the descent. Meanwhile, those left behind to wait, went on about their usual activities. The parade, led by the local band, dinner at the church tent, or picnic suppers brought from home. Men went off to the judging of the animals; women to the exhibition hall to watch the judging of produce.

Children were never given freer rein. What could happen to them at a country fair? Off they'd go to find their own fun, returning to parents only for more money for games of skill or chance. Bingo, the shooting gallery, tossing rings, throwing baseballs! Happy whether they won a thin metal ring with a large stone, or a big stuffed monkey.

For me it was the merry-go-round or ferris wheel. How I loved them! Five cents a ride. Or, if ten cents, then three for a quarter. Though my mother would try to get me to sit in a seat on the merry-go-round with my little brother, so she would not need to ride, I, self-willed as always, would ride a horse, playing the big lady. How I loved it when they stopped the ferris wheel while I was at the top, surveying the whole fairgrounds below! And the rides, they were never long enough. "Oh, can't I go round just one more time," I'd plead when they'd stop the wheel to let me off.

For my parents, sitting in the grandstand, it was the harness races, the spirited horses, the jockeys in their gay caps and blouses, leaning forward, legs straddled, feet on the shafts. Father never bet but if there was one place he'd get excited it was at the races.

No one went home until it was learned where the balloon had landed. I have no memory of any fatalities. Men might come out bruised and a bit battered, but they always came out. Neither man nor balloon was beyond repair

SCHOOL DAYS

I've often claimed that, growing up in a time far before busing, that I'd walked to school all my life. That statement isn't exactly true; I have vague memories of going to what must have been preschool classes. A group of friends and I were tutored, tended, and coddled by a young woman in an upper room of her house. As this was better than a mile from my home, I was taken there by horse and buggy, which, I guess, has to be considered the equivalent of busing.

I dimly remember kindergarten as being a large room with lots of small chairs which I loved and low tables on which we drew pictures with crayons on paper and built things with many colored blocks.

What I remember best is that the first two or three days of school were generally anguish to me. Everything was so strange and different from home, and I got very homesick.

I don't remember my first grade teacher at all.

What made school bearable, was our music teacher; a large heavy-set man with a wonderful voice, he sang at church and at town celebrations. He was a friend of my parents, and I felt at home with him. I loved the songs he taught us: "Good Morning, Merry Sunshine," "My Bonnie Lies Over the Ocean, bring back my Bonnie to me, to me." I remember how I used to have to work to reach that last high "me".

"Two Little Girls in Blue, Lad." For years I thought that last word was lead, and I couldn't see why such a heavy thing as lead could be in a song. Best of all I loved it when the teacher divided the room into three sections and had us sing "rounds". "Row, Row, Row Your Boat", that was always fun.

I'll never forget my second grade teacher. She was young, pretty, kind, and I, like everyone in the class, adored her. Just as an example of her understanding; one day I was wearing to school a new undergarment, a sort of vest-like garment that buttoned down the front with garters to hold up my stockings. I had never had any underwear like this before and I was so proud of it I had to share my joy of it with someone. So I went up to the teacher's desk, in a whisper told her about this wonderful garment and asked if she'd like to see it. Her enthusiasm, when she said she would, elated me.

We went out into the long coat closet hall, I lifted my dress to display my new pride and joy and her enthusiastic praise of this simple article of clothing doubled my love of her. She was such a beloved and loving teacher I'll never forget her.

Only one incident do I recall about my third grade but it was an event that filled my heart with joy. My Mother came to a school program in which I had an important part. Generally Mother had just had a baby, or was going to have one, or some hotel duty made it impossible for her to visit school and how often it hurt that among mothers who came to visit school my own mother was not there.

But no child was ever happier than I to have her mother in the audience than I was that day, though she was then well along in pregnancy, which fact I did not learn of till years later. But I knew then that when I became a mother I would go to everything I could in which my children had a part!

The fourth grade I remember especially for how we used to vie with one another to stay after school to erase the blackboards, to have them clean for next day. I felt very proud when the honor came to me. But one day it wasn't an honor at all. Remember those little inkwells we used to have on the right hand corner of our desks, and the steel pens we wrote with?

Well, one day, instead of writing with the pens, a friend who sat across the aisle from me and I began spattering each other with ink. By the time the teacher, who'd been teaching B class, noticed us, we were a mess.

So we had to remain after school and write on the board, "I will never spatter ink again" for 50 times. This was a common schoolroom punishment in those days. After we had finished our punishment we had to erase the board clean—there was little honor in the task on this occasion.

One time when one of my best intentions went awry was when I was in room 7. I'd wanted to be in this room for a long time; it was way up under the eaves with dormer windows, but it was taught by a lovely woman whose name was Merrill and I thought it would be nice to be taught by someone with my last name.

In this room at the school performance I spoke a piece only one line of which I remember: "Spink, Spank, Spink." Anyway, I did everything I could to be on my good behavior. Or so I thought.

Around this time the soles of children's shoes were covered with leather that was pasted down outside the stitching. When it worked loose, kids used to pull that outer edging off. One day I saw a girl across the aisle doing this very thing. As her mother worked at the hotel I knew they were poor people with a large family and out of the goodness of my heart—please believe me—I wrote her a note telling her that I felt she shouldn't pull her shoes apart as her father must have a hard time supplying the family with shoes.

Having what I thought was her welfare at heart, it was heart-breaking to have her betray me. Anyway, I was kept after school, and the teacher showed me the note I had written to this girl.

In surprise, I tried to explain how I thought I'd been doing a kind deed. Fortunately the teacher believed me, but she gave me a little talk on how I should be careful about hurting other people's feelings.

I lived five long blocks from school and until I was ten years old, I walked those blocks four times a day. For we had no warm lunches then so all kids went home to dinner. I always had one terror to face on my way home. Every day a certain boy would jump out from some store opening and chase me home. I was frightened to death of him and ran sobbing and sobbing until within a block of the hotel, he let me go.

Finally my teacher wormed it out of me why I hated going home, and after that my troubles with that bully ceased.

My mother, being unaware of those unhappy first days of school each fall, always said that I liked school, and that she never had any trouble making me go. She was right there, until I went into the fifth grade. That teacher was the only one I ever had that I disliked. She was cross and mean. I both feared and disliked her, as did most of her pupils, I feel safe in saying. Looking back, I see her as a frustrated old maid who, wanting to be married, hated teaching and took it out on us kids.

Punishing pupils was permissible in those days. Spankings were common, and parents never interfered. In fact, many a parent warned his offspring if he got a flogging at school, he could expect another when he got home. Generally an unruly boy was sent to the principal's office, and many a time I have cringed in hearing the yells emitting from behind the door of the principal's office as some kid was "getting his."

Some teachers did their own flogging. The custom was to take a child out into the cloak hall, shut the door, and take the pointer to him. His unhappy yells were something the rest of the class didn't like to hear, and doubtless kept us on better behavior than we would have been otherwise.

One day, this teacher that I so disliked determined to make her whipping more impressive, took the pointer to a boy in front of the whole class and his screams must have been heard over the entire building. He was a big boy whose mother worked for us at the hotel, and I knew that his family was poor. I liked both the boy and his mother, and finally, unable to listen any longer to his screams, I jumped up from my seat and cried out, "You stop whipping that boy. He didn't do anything so bad, and if you don't stop whipping him, I'll tell my father!"

Why I brought my father into the situation, I have no idea. But probably no teacher was ever more surprised at a pupil's action, and from sheer surprise, I imagine, she stopped and told me to take my seat, informing me, "I'll tend to you after school, young lady!"

She only gave me a stern talking to. But I begged my mother after that to have me put into another room, either lower or higher, I didn't care which. I just put up a big fuss about going back to that room. Nevertheless, I had to go, but my mother did protest to the principal about a child being punished in front of the entire room, and after that things were better.

The most usual punishment was a slap with a ruler on an open hand. Since I was both a good and obedient pupil, who sought the teacher's favor by trying to please her, always in the A class, I slipped through school without any punishment, except on one occasion.

I had a fortune telling fish, about an inch and a half long, made out of a sort of slippery paper. When it was held on an open palm, the warmth of a hand made it curl up, and the manner in which it curled— according to directions printed on the fish—told one's fortune. One day I was demonstrating it to the boy across the aisle from me. We were both turned so we were facing each other, our heads very close together over my open hand.

The teacher, who was attending to the B class, spoke to us across the room, telling us to turn around in our seats. We did as she asked, but very cagily I still held my hand out in the aisle, low enough to be out of the teacher's sight, so the boy could see the fish curl. But I wasn't as smart as I thought. Before I had time to pull in my hand, the teacher was there beside us and instead of holding a paper fish, the palm of my hand was feeling the sharp blows of her ruler.

But that teacher I liked better than any I'd ever had. Each morning before we began classes, she'd read us a chapter from some popular children's book. That certainly was a good way to make sure we got to school on time! Not one word of that story did I want to miss. Not only did I enjoy the story, but it filled my young heart with ambition. One day when walking home from school with a playmate, discussing the book the teacher was reading, I said, "When I get big, I'm going to write a book, too."
"Oh," she exclaimed scornfully, "you'll never be smart enough to write a book."

Evidently I believed her, for my aspirations in that direction were temporarily squelched. But they bobbed up again at a time when I was reading "The Youth's Companion," and "St. Nicholas Magazine," publications then popular with children, I began sending stories to them.

Result? Rejection slips! I never did see anything of mine in print until I went away to boarding school and had things in the school paper. But by that time I was writing under the supervision of good teachers.

CHRISTMAS REMEMBERED

What a place for a child to be on Christmas Eve – on a dusty, dimly lighted train speeding through the night. That was years and years ago, but I can still feel the bumpety-bump, bumpety-bump, and hear the clickety-click, clickety-clack of the wheels as they ran swiftly over the uneven rails. I can hear the mournful wooOOoo—wooOOoo of the whistle sending out its urgent warning, "Get off the track people. We're coming through!"

Everyone was sleeping, heads nodding, everything still but for the muffled sound of voices carrying on a muted conversation. The sudden outcry of a sleepy child, hushed into quick silence by his mother. I see the brakeman weaving down the aisle, giving himself to the movement of the train, lantern in his hand, cap set cockily on his head as he bawls out the name of one stop (scarcely more than a farm elevator on a lonesome prairie) between my grandparent's home and ours. I was homeward bound. I'd been visiting my grandparents, and now they were taking me home for Christmas.

My grandmother, her tall gaunt figure hidden under her long dark cape, her small bonnet tied under her chin with narrow black velvet ribbons, sat stern and aloof on the dusty red plush seat beside me. Facing me sat my grandfather, jolly as Santa himself, and as ruddy of cheek. No white whiskers, though; just a droopy black mustache. No funny red cap on his head, only a shiny bald spot which, in the murky glow that fell from the lantern-like light fixtures that swayed from the ceiling, looked shinier that ever. Most important of all, always, that merry twinkle in his little black eyes.

I was worried because there was no snow. The ground outside the speeding train was bare and black. And I couldn't possibly see how Santa's eight reindeer could go leaping from rooftop to rooftop if there was no snow. "How's Santa Claus going to get here Grandma," I kept pestering her, "if it doesn't snow?"

I'm sure she must have given me a reassuring answer. If not, I know that my grandfather would have. Some quip, perhaps to ease my childish concern and to make me smile a little. Yet, I kept turning back to the darkened window, pressing my face against the cold pane, shading my eyes with my hands, seeking vainly for the sight of even one snowflake. All I saw was the shadowy form of farm buildings flashing by...barns, tall ghostly telephone poles, animals standing motionless in a pasture, the smudge of trees, the sheen of black water as the train rattled over a trestle.

All that is still very clear to me, but whether or not snow came that night I don't remember, for when I was carried from the train I was sound asleep, and when I awakened Christmas morning, I was snug and warm in my own bed. Too excited to even think of snow, for a tall glittering tree, all asparkle with candlelight, and a mound of beribboned packages beneath it, assured me that, snow or no snow, Santa had come!

Odd, isn't it, how some childhood memories are as deeply etched on our minds as if the event that gave them birth had happened only yesterday, while others have sunk so deeply into the pit of forgetfulness that only an analyst could dig them out. The happenings of that Christmas morning are entirely gone, while the vividness of that train ride, my fear that there would be no snow for Santa, are indelibly etched on my mind.

My childhood Christmases, all of which were spent in my parents' hotel, were happy ones, but memories of them, somehow have all melted like a handful of crayons left on a hot stove, and run together into one colorful whole. All our pre-Christmas activities took place in a "Transient" room, directly across the hall from our family room. Although my parents, the maids, and any adult could go freely in and out of that room, to us children it was definitely off limits.

That rule still didn't prevent our trying to peek, hanging around in the hall, hoping to get a glimpse of the magic that went on behind that door, as those more privileged than we went in and out. That any tree, or bicycle, or doll carriage could get into that room without being seen by our eagle eyes is unbelievable; but Christmas morning gave proof that they certainly had, and made all our waiting worthwhile.

One Christmas I well remember Junie spent the night with me. She was Jewish and celebrated Chanukah; the excitement of Christmas Eve was new to her, and what a time we had getting to sleep! We tried hard enough as we'd been warned that Santa wouldn't come while we were awake, so eventually we dozed off. But not for long! Some slight noise at the foot of our bed awakened us. In our highly excited state, even the skittering of a mouse would have done the trick!

The room was in darkness except for a slender ray of light falling through a partly opened door. That light fell softly over a tree being put in place and we saw someone moving. Nothing in the world could have convinced us that this wasn't Santa Claus getting ready to trim our tree, and never did two pigtailed heads duck back under covers more quickly lest Santa discovered we were awake, and so disappear.

We awakened Christmas morning and saw a fully decorated tree: Santa had stayed and finished his job!

Our Christmas trees were always ceiling high, and excitingly beautiful: aglitter with tinsel, delicate baubles of gold and silver, asparkle with tiny wax candles that kept tipping over, or that had to be blown out and replaced. Even though we might recognize those strings of popcorn and cranberries on the tree as those we had strung a few days before, never did we doubt but that Santa had put them there. For hadn't Mother told us we were stringing them so they'd be ready for Santa, as he wouldn't have time to stop and string them himself?

The splendor of the Christmas tree was rivaled only by the heaps of tissue-wrapped presents beneath! A bisque doll with real hair, eyes that could be opened and closed (and a small brother could poke out!), a set of real China dishes, an iron and ironing board to play house with, and an honest-to-goodness iron stove in which I could build a real fire and bake tiny biscuits.

Junie's mother had made us each identical beautiful little robes, with crocheted slippers to match. Junie and I donned our robes and slippers immediately, and wore them the whole time we were opening our presents. And, believe me, it was hard to get us out of them!

WE'VE COME A LONG WAY, BABY!

I never really did swallow the stork story. Instead, I believed that our dear Dr. Whitley brought Mother's babies in his little black bag. Yet, this explanation wasn't entirely satisfactory, and soon I began to wonder, "Where does he get them?" So I boldly asked, "Where do babies come from?" and was told "You'll learn when you're older."

One day, when playing in my playhouse in the backyard, I wandered over to the barn to talk to our yardman, George, who was currying the horses that drew the baggage drays to the depot and back. George, like most of our help, was always nice with us kids. As he was brushing the long black tail of one of the horses, I asked, "George, how do you tell a mama from a papa horse?" I can still see him redden, then stammer, "You'll find out when you grow older." The stock reply!

I grew older very slowly! One day I was playing at the house of a small schoolmate when her mother, a friend of Mother's, came into the room. "Well, Irene," she said, "How are you, and how's your mother?" Whatever I answered, I don't know. I could only blurt out, "My Mrs. Daley, but you're getting fat!" She laughed and agreed, "I guess I am."

A few nights later I was having supper over at Junie's. I liked to eat at their house because right under Mrs. Oppenheimer's place at the table was a small button which, when she stepped on it, brought the maid from the kitchen to see what she wanted. I likened it to the appearance of the genii from the lamp, and thought it to be magic.

This night at the table were Junie's parents, her father, a meek little man, and her mother, a short, heavy set woman with startlingly black hair and eyes; boss of all she surveyed, even her husband. Also Julius, the Oppenheimer's nineteen year old nephew who had come from Germany to learn the men's clothing business from his uncle, was there.

Somehow, Mrs. Daley was mentioned and I, childlike, wanting to get into conversation, blurted out, "My! Is she ever getting fat! I was over at her house the other day and she could hardly walk." Unaware of any reaction to the remark, I went right on eating.

But the next day Mrs. Oppenheimer bustled over to the hotel and into my mother's rooms with an indignant, "Mrs. Merrill, you've got to tell Irene about babies." After repeating my remark of the night before, she added, "Poor Julius!" There he sat, squirming, his face red as a beet, not knowing where to look. Irene is old enough to know these things and you're absolutely wrong in not telling her."

This I never learned until long afterwards. Sometime later I was over at Mrs. Daley's and she took me into her bedroom to show me two darling babies in a crib. I didn't connect this with her sudden slimness!

Mother hadn't followed Mrs. Oppenheimer's advice. In those days, with few exceptions, mother's were not wise enough to enlighten their children on this subject. We learned about sex from schoolmates, generally in unpleasant ways so that we grew up believing it to be something shameful.

So different in the "gay nineties" and at the turn of the century! Sex was a dirty word, never spoken in mixed company, and only in whispers between ladies. An unwed mother was ostracized; a teacher in our

194

town who had a baby (and seldom, if ever, did we have married teachers) was unable to get a teaching job afterwards. One good, moral, church-going mother turned her own daughter out of the house when she learned she was pregnant, and she nor anyone else ever heard of that girl again, or what became of her.

An illegitimate child was also black-listed and no parent wanted their son or daughter to marry one, unfair as that may seem. "Affair" was then an unknown word. You might say a man had an affinity, which was the same as meaning a mistress, but such goings on were kept secret. If a boy kept a girl out overnight for any reason whatsoever, although it might be quite innocent, he had "compromised" her, and the decent thing to do was to marry her. Girls and boys were not supposed to kiss, hold hands, or in any way embrace, unless they were engaged. And naturally, women must be fully clothed, not even an ankle showing!

Pregnant was a word not used; it was "she's in the family way." And while that should have been no disgrace if one were married, it was treated as if it were, and women would go to all lengths to keep their condition hidden until a bulging figure made it impossible to be concealed any longer. And women were always trying to guess if another in her clan were "that way." "Do you think she is?" They'd say of someone who was suspect. "I think she looks like it."

The delay in my education, perhaps, was due to the protection of an older cousin, Florence[46], who came to live with us when her mother, my mother's sister, died. Wise in such things herself, she shielded me. But one day I was with her and a group of her friends when one of the girls began to tell a story. Florence, with a warning look in my direction, cut her off and the girl ended the tale in such a way that I knew something funny was going on. Later, I began pestering Florence to open up.

She resisted at first, but when I threatened to tell mother what had happened, she broke down and told me what today we call "the facts of life," warning me, "Don't tell your mother I told you."

My new knowledge depressed me, and my enlightenment was more embarrassing than beneficial. But, fortunately, with children, unhappy moods don't linger long. With home and school activities claiming my attention, gradually the matter of sex sank into a place of unimportance in my mind.

Yet, in my youth, sex was never spoken of in a mixed society. If mentioned among women, in the recounting of some scandal, it was whispered, with a furtive look around, lest they be overheard.

Some time ago, comparing morals of my day with those of today with a young college boy, he said, "I don't suppose you'd ever let anyone see you kiss." "See us kiss!" I scoffed, "We didn't kiss!"

A slight exaggeration I admit. More accurately, "We were not supposed to kiss." Certainly not until we were engaged. I recall an incident which, compared to today's morals, seems actually comic. A group of middle-aged women, picnicking in the woods, came upon a young couple standing on a swinging bridge over a small stream, rapturously kissing each other. Respectable people hearing the story were scandalized! Happily, the reputation of the transgressors was saved when, shortly afterward, they were married.

Later, women from that same group went to Chicago as delegates of some club. On returning home, they told of a scandalous show they had seen in which scantily dressed women danced on tables, drank wine, and smoked cigarettes --- many years before women smoked. Of the three "sins" these women witnessed, they held smoking to be the worst.

Early in my boarding school days, around the turn of the century, I visited a schoolmate in a college town. In crossing the park one evening, I was shocked to see boys and girls strolling along, arms around each other. Displaying affection in <u>any</u> way in those days just wasn't done, but when I mentioned this to my friend she said, nonchalantly, "Oh, those were college kids. They do it all the time."

I also recall when one of the major women's magazines (Companion, the Journal) printed an article entitled, "Sex is Fun!" Expressing such an idea in that generation was so far out of line that the article was considered obscene, and many women canceled their subscriptions.

Much of what I have written I learned from listening to conversations between my mother and her friends. Should one of them notice my absorption in their conversation, she would be sure to say, "Little pitchers have big ears." And there was a quick change of conversation. Which seemed a ridiculous remark to me since little girls had ears, not pitchers.

But Mother's friends needn't have worried. Much of what I overheard was more puzzling than informative. It was many years before rules governing the morals of young girls were relaxed. A non-virgin was presumed to be damaged goods that few men would marry. A young lady who had an illegitimate child was considered "ruined for life," and was practically ostracized. This happened to a school teacher in our town who everyone had always liked. Naturally she lost her job. What became of her after that, whether or not she kept her child, I don't know, but I do remember one remark she is said to have made, "This is what comes of petting on the living room davenport!"

A tragedy which occurred when I was still an infant, but about which rumors never died involved a young lady who was turned away from home by her mother when she found her daughter was pregnant. As rumor had it, the mother never again heard from her daughter, never knew what became of her. The mother was a good church-going Christian woman, highly respected in the community. At the time I knew her she worked, voluntarily, helping the poor, doing much good. Today we would call her a social worker; in those days, of course, there was no such thing as organized social work.

So far as I know, the word "pregnant" was never used in referring to a woman "with child." The accepted expression, which for some reason I never liked, was "in the family way." But, believe me, a woman kept her condition secret until secrecy was no longer possible. For a woman in her "delicate condition" to be seen in public was considered improper, so most women kept confined to their homes for the last six months of pregnancy.

Women were always trying to discover if some woman was "that way." "Is she?" or "Isn't she?" they'd wonder among themselves. I once overheard my mother tell of a time when her group of young couples were enjoying a dinner at one of their homes. In doing up the dishes afterwards, the hostess kept taking her hands out of the dishpan to go to the bathroom. A suspicious sign! So the others began surmising, "She must be!" She was.

Following childbirth, a woman was kept in bed two weeks. This was considered necessary to allow displaced organs to settle back in place. With a RN, or perhaps a practical nurse taking care of her and the whole family, this might afford a woman the only rest she got in a year or better. Until, perhaps, a couple of years later another confinement came along for her to "enjoy."

"Affairs" or lust for the other man's wife existed, but only under the strictest secrecy. Instead of describing such a condition as "an affair," a man and woman "had an affinity" for each other, but the attachment, while it might be surmised, was all very hush-hush. Once out in the open, a couple was socially ostracized.

A divorce was considered a disgrace, a divorcee or "grass widow" held in low opinion; so women often would long endure intolerable conditions before submitting to a divorce. When an uncle of mine divorced his wife, Mother was deeply upset, bemoaning the fact that this was the first divorce there'd ever been in the family.

But that marriage was wrong from the start, engineered by my overly ambitious grandmother. Aunt Lucy's father was wealthy, important, and one of the town's founders, so Grandmother thought this would be a wonderful marriage for her son. Aunt Lucy herself was a kind, gentle, unpretentious woman, and she loved my uncle dearly, but she was considerably older than he, and the marriage just didn't work out.

Auntie Mae,[47] my uncle's second wife, was a widow and as different from Aunt Lucy as a butterfly from a moth. Vivacious, effusive, a "frilly" dresser, she was a retired milliner, and a bleached blonde, which were two strikes against her in our small town! But, friendly and outgoing, she was an asset to her husband's hotel business. Though seemingly a successful marriage for many years, it too ended in divorce.

A married woman working outside the home was taboo. A man considered it a slight on his earning power, and no man wanted to be known as unable to provide for his family. Never were the words, "A woman's place is in the home" more firmly accepted.

Jobs for single young women were practically nonexistent. Teaching was her best choice, as teachers were looked up to and accepted socially. But a teacher had to walk the straight and narrow path. Cards, late hours, dancing, were often banned. Men, therefore, looked other places for company so the "old maid school teacher" was more than just a name. Most teachers became so; never were married women hired as school teachers. Librarians were also respected, but a town our size didn't have much of a market for librarians!

With the exception of furniture, men's clothing, and drug stores, most clerks were young women. But long hours standing on one's feet, low pay, and little social life, made clerking a dull job. Milliners came under the "merry widow" class, though those in our town were most respectable.

Telephone operators were looked at askew. Perhaps because in our town the owner of the phone system was a gentleman who had a taste for the wrong kind of woman, and was exceptionally good to those who did him "favors."

As to working in a man's office – Ha! When the typewriter became perfected so that it was accepted as a useful business machine, much controversy arose among men as to whether men or women should use it.

Many people believed that men and women must not be employed together in industry because that would lead to sexual irregularities and the breakdown of the country's morals. Yet here was the typewriter and it could be operated by women. Women were more efficient typists and were willing to work for low salaries. There were those people who believed that the six month typing course was too arduous for a woman, and that she would tire sitting at the typewriter all day. No need to comment on the outcome of that! When shorthand came into being and girls became stenographers, there weren't enough secretaries to go around.

Still, the matter of propriety raged. Typists and stenographers did not have a "good name." I once heard a woman remark, puffing herself up like a pouter pigeon, "I would never let a daughter of mine work in a man's office." She had no need for worrying, she never had a daughter! Jealous wives also fought the on rush of women into their husband's offices. But, nothing stemmed the tide; women went to work and have been working hard ever since!

A CONVENT BRED LADY

In my mother's day to be Convent-bred was quite the thing. So this was my mother's wish for me, her first child. Hers was a dream born before her marriage when, as a professional seamstress, she lived and worked in the homes of wealthy Minneapolis families, outfitting their daughters.

In one of these homes were two convent-bred girls who were such delightfully charming young ladies that Mother decided that if she ever had any daughters, she'd want them to be educated in a convent. "Convent-bred young women," Mother told me, "are the kinds of ladies that sit on a pillow and sew a fine seam." I'm sure that I, with my disdain for sewing and my affinity for mischief, reinforced her original idea!

Since we were not Catholic, it might have been difficult for Mother to convince my father this was best for me except that Mother had an ally, the priest in our town. Father O'Brien dined often at our hotel and became a good friend of my father's. One day Mother mentioned to him this dream of hers, and with Father

O'Brien on her side, my father was won over. So that June, when I was ten years old and ready for the

Seventh Grade, the good priest took me to the graduation exercises of St. Clara Academy.[48]

The school was in East Dubuque,[49] and better known as Sinsinawa Mound, Wisconsin, after a real Indian mound that was there. The long three story brick building, fronted by a grove of noble pines and backed by a hillside of more beautiful trees, was most impressive.

Moreover, the commencement exercises, with the girls rushing around in their pretty dresses afterwards, made convent life seem almost glamorous. If Father O'Brien had wanted to win me over, he had done so, and that fall of 1899 he took me back to enter the school where I remained until I was eighteen.

But once I was ensconced in my curtained cubicle, the excitement I had felt in going away to boarding school quickly evaporated. The room was a far cry from the pretty one I had shared with my sisters at home. We slept in curtained alcoves in large dormitories and our "cells", as we called them, with their unattractive wash stands, bowl and pitcher, and narrow cots were cold and un-homelike.

Surrounded by a whirl of girls, not one of whom I knew, the homesickness I'd felt on my first few days at public school was nothing compared to this. My longing for my brother and sisters, my parents and especially the warmth of my mother, was so near intolerable that every night of those first few weeks, I cried myself to sleep.

Nor did I get off to a good start with my friendships. At home my small friends and I had played with beautiful little bisque dolls, with curly blond, black, or brown hair, for which we loved to make clothes. We also converted old orange crates into doll houses outfitted with miniature furniture. Certain that I would find similar playmates at school, against my mother's advice, I insisted on taking my dolls and furniture with me.

An old unused brick church at school had been converted into a trunk house. Here we unpacked and carried our clothes to the attic where each girl had a compartment for her possessions. While I was unpacking, a couple of pieces of doll furniture fell from my trunk onto the floor. The girl who was unpacking next to me saw this, picked up a piece of the furniture and regarded me with a scornful, "Don't tell me that a girl as big as you still plays with dolls?"

No! I didn't admit to it. I just stood for a moment, not knowing what to say and finally came up with the only logical answer. "Well, hardly! Some of my little sister's things must have gotten in my trunk by mistake."

"Oh!" she said. "I thought it was funny." But what a close call! You may be sure of one thing, my doll things stayed in my trunk until I went home in June.

I had another unpleasant experience in that church. Every Thursday afternoon, which was free of classes, the church was unlocked and we had access to our trunks. Occasionally on these Thursdays, I'd sneak up into the choir loft and read. It was quiet there, isolated, sort of a moody atmosphere, and I wouldn't be bothered. One afternoon as it darkened, I came out of my book long enough to become aware that everything was quiet. Looking down into the room below me, I saw that the church door was closed, and not a soul was there.

Well, I was isolated all right. The door was locked and the church far enough from the main building that unless someone were passing nearby, I could yell my head off, rattle the door till it came off the hinges, and no one would hear me. Not until I was missed at supper and a hurried search failed to uncover me, did someone remember they'd seen me in the choir loft and I was rescued.

Naturally shy, not one to make advances, it was some time before I made friends. Seeing old friends rushing effusively into each other's arms, kissing and hugging each other, chattering away together about happenings in their summer vacations, increased my loneliness. Nor did a second encounter with a potential friend turn out well. When she asked my name, I told her. But when she asked my age and I told her, she almost flipped. "Eleven years old," she repeated scathingly. "Don't tell me a girl as big as you are is only that old. That's ridiculous! You must be thirteen years old at least." Right then was the end of what I had hoped might be a beautiful friendship!

Her doubts were understandable. Not only was I tall for my age, but being very thin and wearing floor-length dresses made me seem even taller.

Actually, by the time I was thirteen, I had reached my full height. Like a stalk of bamboo, I sprung up so fast that when I went home that first Christmas, I had so far outgrown my clothes—skirts too short, arms dangling out of my sleeves—that my mother was shocked when she first saw me.

As she later confessed, she even wept a few secret tears at having so ungainly a daughter who was far different from the charming convent-bred daughter she had envisioned. That this is true is borne out by the fact that mother did not try this same experiment with any of my sisters. They all lived at home and attended public school.

Gradually, I made friends. Eventually, I learned there were other lonesome new girls and soon we were mingling with the old as naturally as if we'd always known each other. But it was years before I got over that initial homesickness in returning to school.

I took the train to the convent every fall. From our little Illinois Central Railroad station in Webster City, I traveled some eighty miles by rail to Dubuque. A handyman from the convent would be at the station to deliver me, and my baggage, safely to the convent. Those eighty lonesome miles to school were almost more than I could bear.

"Well, Irene," the ticket agent—a man I'd known all my life, father of one of my small friends—would say as he stamped my ticket, "back to school again?" and I, unable to speak because of that lump in my throat, would only nod as I slid my change and my ticket into my purse.

And it was the same, as I stood beside my father, watching the baggage man check my trunk. "Back to school again, huh, Irene? Someday you'll be so smart, maybe you'll be our first woman president." With misted eyes, I saw the faces of my parents as I waved to them from the window as the train chugged slowly out of the station, leaving them behind.

The second fall after I went away to the convent I

was so lonely that I wrote my father a letter, begging him to let me come back home. Each semester Dad sent me to school with a check for $150. $120 was for tuition; the remainder was put in the Sister's care for any incidentals I might have to buy. I wrote Dad that I hadn't given my check to the Sisters yet so he wouldn't lose any money if I were to return home.

It was the custom of the Sisters to read all incoming and outgoing mail. My pitiful plea was read and I was called into the office. Gently I was persuaded to turn over my check; the Sisters convincing me it was not safe for me to carry around such a large amount of money. The Sisters promised that should my father let me come home, the check would be returned to me intact. Father's answer to my letter, as I should have anticipated, was a firm <u>no</u>!

Which was as it should have been. For once those first few weeks of homesickness were past, I did enjoy boarding school. It was not all study. We did have fun. On Valentine's day, Thanksgiving and other special occasions the Sisters would hire an orchestra from Dubuque (Iowa) and we'd have a dance. Naturally, we had only girls to dance with, but we had fun. At lest once a month some celebrity would come to entertain us: speaker, musician, elocutionist, even Paderewski. One elocutionist, I remember, recited Enoch Arden with such emotion that I wept all through it. Since then I've always been partial to books, movies, and plays that leave me with red eyes and a sodden handkerchief, that I thoroughly enjoyed.

Each fall after grapes and apples had been gathered, we were turned loose in the vineyard and orchard to pick the leavings and how we loved that! We could play golf, tennis, and basketball. What an asset my height was there! As our baskets were not regulation height, I could practically reach up and drop the ball into the baskets, so in choosing up sides, I was often the first picked.

Once winter began, coasting became my favorite activity. Sitting on our sleds, we'd start at the top of a long flight of stairs and go bumping down over the steps, across the driveway, and down through the pines. Our ride was made faster by the bed of slippery pine needles which lay beneath the snow. We had to steer our sleds through a narrow gate at the foot of the hill, or we would crash into a barbed wire fence. Once a priest, who was coasting with us, did run into the fence, and only the quick digging in of his heels when he saw where he was headed, broke the impact and kept him from serious injury.

As we guided our sleds mainly by digging in our heels, our shoes took a beating. Mother was always appalled at the condition of my shoes when I came home each spring, as the heels were almost devoid of leather. A fact that never bothered me.

Occasionally an unexpected and certainly forbidden pleasure enlivened our usual placid life. For example, one St. Valentine's Day, a bunch of boys from St. Joseph's College, Dubuque, hired horses and buggies and drove out to the school to have a little fun, and invited some of the girls to go buggy-riding. Even the fear of certain punishment couldn't keep the girls from accepting such an invitation. They simply piled into the buggies and off they went. Because of my young age, this didn't particularly interest me, but very few of the older girls refused the invitation.

Those poor nuns! If you've ever seen a flustered hen trying to gather a bunch of unruly chicks back under her wings, you may have some idea of their helplessness. It was late afternoon before the boys dropped the girls off at the convent gates—doubtless afraid to come nearer—and took off.

Certainly some punishment, tho' I don't know what kind, was meted out to the miscreants. But when one of the girls on the following day said to one of the nuns, "Yesterday was certainly a red letter day, wasn't it, Sister?" the reply was, "It certainly was. Letters have been read, are being read, and will be read!" Because all convent mail was censored, many of the girls had taken the opportunity of their buggy ride to send letters to their boy friends. Yet, in spite of the girls' attempts, the nuns had somehow gotten possession of those letters!

But sad things happened, too. One evening I was called out of study hour. Mother Superior wanted to see me in the library. To be called before Mother Superior was serious. As I left my seat, I began to wonder what I might have done wrong. The nun was sitting solemnly behind a big desk. She motioned me to a chair in front of it. "Now, Irene," she said as I sat down, "I want you to be a brave little girl."

Immediately I turned cold with fear as I thought that something terrible must have happened at home. I could hardly get the words out of my mouth, "My mother?" "No! No, Irene," she said, "Not your mother." So I gasped out, "My father?"

I've often thought, "If only she'd have told me straight out." I went through such anguish wondering what it could be before she told me that my baby brother had died, shortly after he had been born. The only emotion that I felt was one of vast relief. I'd never seen that baby. I'd not even known my mother was expecting a baby. As I returned to the study hall, I tried to feel sad but couldn't make it. Mother Superior had dismissed me with, "Go write your mother a nice letter."

Looking back to the letter I wrote now, I think, "How unfeeling can a child be?" That letter was never mentioned between us, but I've often wondered what Mother thought when she read it. I've forgotten just how I worded it, and I did tell her I was sorry. But then I wrote something to the affect, "Don't grieve too badly. That baby might have grown up to be a mean criminal and caused you lots of sorrow. Maybe it's better this way." I remember thinking I was so noble, that my words were so consoling. It is unlikely that my mother shared my feeling.

This was my Victor Hugo phase. I'd been reading a set of his books belonging to my mother and one fall I took Les Miserables back to school with me, and I kept it in my desk. Inspired by his genius, I was writing stories about sad children, bad children, abused, starving, dying children, or any other morbid subject I could think of. I can still see, as if they were right before me now, some of the doleful pictures in that book.

One day the book was missing. I spoke to my teacher about it. "Oh, yes," said the nun. "I have it. I feel that is not proper reading for a child of your age. I'll return it when you go home." It was some time before I got back to Victor.

Occasionally a bunch of us would gang up in some girl's cell, sprawled out on the bed, the floor, or perching on a wide window sill, and attempt to solve the world's problems, or at least discuss them. However, without a radio it was difficult to keep up with what was going on outside convent walls. But I remember the time the Wright brothers were trying out their wings down at Kitty Hawk.

"Well, I hope they don't succeed," spoke up one girl from the corner where she was huddled on the floor. "Because somewhere in the Bible it says that when men fly like birds, the world will come to an end."

Whether or not the Bible says that, I don't know, but it may; I haven't read every word in that book. However, one girl quickly came up with the pronouncement, "Well, men never will fly like birds. They'll always need gasoline and birds don't." However, what with gliding, or hopping off hilltops on a set of wings, I'm not too sure she was right.

Automobiles, too, had just begun to appear. Whenever a girl returned in the fall with the announcement that her father owned an automobile, she immediately acquired a new status. So when a girl returned to inform us that her family owned TWO cars, one for her mother and one for her father, we immediately thought they must be millionaires. And in those days a millionaire was as awe-inspiring as a billionaire is today. It was the rare mother of any of us that even had her own horse'n buggy. She was privileged to use the family rig only when Master didn't want it. Even my mother had to wait till the baggage horse wasn't busy so that she could go riding. For some time, horses would be our main means of transportation. A team and carryall would for many years be transporting the girls from the train in Dubuque to the convent.

Though special uniforms were not required at the convent, we had to wear navy blue dresses on week days and black on Sundays. Since dresses could be made in any style, I usually inveigled my mother in making my Sunday dresses quite fancy. One year however, at my request, my everyday dresses were so plain that on me they must have been dreadful to look at. They were severely plain, floor length, with high collars and long sleeves. Always dark blue.

Our waitresses wore what was then known as princess dresses. They had beautiful figures. Self-made, perhaps, as in those days of iron stay corsets a woman could have almost any figure she desired. The dresses were floor length and fit the woman's self-made figure so snugly that they appeared to have been poured into them.

By pulling strings, she could have a wasp-like waist so that she seemed almost cut in two in the middle. Since flesh displaced in such a manner had to go someplace, it generally went into the enlargement of her bosom. If she were still not pleased with the result, ruffles or inflatable rubber bras could add some inches. Bustles of any shape or size effectively enlarged hips or fannies. Accented by small, fetching, ruffled, white aprons, the waitresses' outfits presented so alluring a picture to my young eyes, that I insisted that my Sunday dresses be of the same style.

Vainly my mother protested: "You need a figure to wear a dress like that Irene, and you still have no figure. You get upset when people call you a bean pole, and that description of you would certainly be justified if you were to wear such a dress." But I insisted, and my mother, as usual, gave in to my desire. I went back to school the proud owner of two black princess dresses! I can't recall the effect the dresses had on my friends, I'm certain that if my figure were eye-catching it was not in the way I'd hoped.

On Saturday afternoons, after we'd had our weekly baths, we were allowed to dress however we pleased. Almost, that is; we had to stay within the bounds of modesty! At that time, a popular outfit was white organdy shirt waists worn with floor length skirts. Under these shirt waists were worn very fancy embroidery "corset covers," with two or three rows of colored baby ribbon woven through the embroidery eyelets.

It was considered chic to have the dainty baby ribbons on the corset cover show through the thin organdy of your blouse. But the nuns would have none of it! If we insisted on wearing organdy shirt waists, then we were required to wear something plain under them. Even the fancy embroidery, without the ribbon, was forbidden.

Often on our free Thursday afternoons (there was no school then), two nuns might take a group of us on a trip over to Menemonee,[50] a small town a few miles from school. Menemonee was composed of little more than a general store and a post office but here we could stock up on candy, fruits and other things unavailable

215

at the convent. We loved this break in the monotony of our daily routine and though we might come home with lagging feet, dusty, disheveled and exhausted, we also came home loaded with goodies which would last for many days ahead.

Smoking, here as everywhere at this time, was a girl's worst sin. On one of these afternoon trips some of the girls bought cigarettes. As some of the girls had private rooms, they gathered in one of them to smoke. Foolish were they in failing to realize that smoke can filter through the smallest crack and that the smell of cigarette can scarcely be disguised. Thus the nuns were able to "smoke" them out and as a punishment they were suspended and sent home for a month.

Sometimes on our free Thursday afternoons or on Saturdays, a carryall, pulled by a team of gentle horses, would take a group of girls, always accompanied by two nuns, all the way into Dubuque to shop. We had to sign up in advance, but once in town we were free to do pretty much as we pleased with the only requirement being that we meet at a certain time and place to go back to school.

One place we always visited was the candy factory. Here we would stock up on slabs of taffy. These slabs were about a foot and a half in length, perhaps half as wide, and came in pink, white or chocolate taffy. Or my favorites, peanut brittle or cocoanut brittle.

Back at school, we'd carry the taffy down to the sweet-press, a small pantry in which we'd keep whatever goodies we bought in town or that were sent us from home. These sweets were available only one hour a day—between the end of classes at four o'clock and study hour at five, so we generally kept one slab of candy under our mattresses where it would be available whenever we wished. Since that was naturally against rules.

The hiding place was a precarious one as the taffy was apt to crackle when we sat or lay on our bed and thus lead a Sister (one slept in every dormitory) to the hidden taffy. Fortunately, since my cell or alcove was at the far end on the room from the Sister's bed I didn't worry much about being discovered.

On one of those shopping tours, one of the girls had not appeared at the appointed time. Finally the nuns took their charges home, then returned to take up the search. She never was found. But what excitement reigned when we learned that by prearrangement—I wonder how with the censoring of our mail she managed that—the girl had met her fiancé in town and they had eloped.

We always had to pay toll to cross the bridge over the Mississippi and there was a legend about that which always amused us. It seems that in the beginning a young and spritely miss stopped at the toll gate to ask the cost. It being a dull day, the gate keeper, wanting to prolong his encounter with this attractive young lady, drawled speculatively, "Well, for a man and a horse the cost is..." Having no wish to banter, the girl said pertly, "Well, this is a maid and a mare," and with a flick of her whip she sent her steed on her way while the gate keeper watching her go, only laughed.

As I was courteous, obedient and a good student, I got along well with all the Sisters. But times came when the monotony of our days so wore me down that I had to take off in some direction and so the occasion of the dough face.

In all probability, you haven't an inkling of what a dough face might have been. Flour and water were mixed to a consistency of pie dough and rolled out to about the same thickness. After that, two slits were made for the eyes, one for the nose, and a larger one for a mouth. Using this as a mask, it was held in place by a sheet which covered the whole body and was pinned around the face. The result was a frightful and ghostly apparition which is hard to imagine.

We somehow had managed to sneak some flour out of the kitchen, and as we had no rolling pin, we had to pat the dough into the right shape. My companions in prankishness knew the habits of our dormitory nuns, that once their charges were in bed, lights out, would go to the chapel for nightly prayers. As soon as we knew they were quietly praying, we went around in our ghastly costumes and stuck our heads in between the curtains of the other girls' cells. Enough light fell from the hall lamps to make our faces perfectly visible to those we visited, and we didn't have to make many calls before the entire dormitory was screaming.

We were near enough the chapel for the Sisters to hear the commotion. By the time our Sister reached our dorm my friend and I were back in our cells, safely tucked in bed, our dough faces hidden. But enough of the girls had recognized us, and we were called on the carpet. The nuns had only one form of punishment. With a sorrowful shake of their heads they said, "Of all people to do such a thing, Irene, I would not believe it of you. I've always trusted you and I'm deeply disappointed. Now go to bed and we'll see what can be done about this in the morning."

Simple words, but said in such a tone that I felt like a whipped dog slinking away with his tail between his

218

legs. Knowing I had committed one of the seven cardinal sins, I behaved myself for a long time after that! Yet, I remember that as I settled down under my covers that night, hiding my shame, there was a tinge of satisfaction in the fun we had had. And whenever my fellow conspirators and I had occasion to reminisce on this adventure, it was with a grin and a touch of smugness.

Things were always happening to increase my education. One day two supposedly friends of mine asked if I'd ever tasted Indian turnip. I hadn't the slightest idea of what it might be, so they handed me a slice of what looked like white turnip and invited me to partake. Always eager to try new things, I partook.

And immediately thought my mouth was on fire. For the hottest thing I ever put in my mouth couldn't compete with that. It stung, it burned, it made me sick. Worse yet, it lasted and lasted! Never a pain had I experienced that had the endurance of that one. I went to sleep that night with my mouth still burning.

But was I a tattler? Did I run to the Sisters? No! I set out to learn what Indian turnip is. A time might come when I, having someone who'd done wrong by me, might want to use it. Have you any idea what I found out? It's the root of the Jack in the Pulpit. The Indians used it for food. But they boiled it and cooking it takes away the burn. So you see, there was a valuable piece of information to add to my wild food lore. If I were ever lost in the woods, Jack in the Pulpit could save me from starving to death. Well boiled, of course.

The Sisters made sure we got a good education at the convent. And I, for the most part, enjoyed my studies. I had little taste for languages, math, or science, but literature and writing class well made up for my dislike of any other subjects.

I had always loved to read, and the nuns introduced me to the great writers in history. I remember studying Homer, Virgil, Sophocles, Euripides, Spenser, Chaucer, Milton, Shakespeare, Jonson! I especially loved the Romantic poets – Blake, Wordsworth, Coleridge, Shelley, Keats, and Byron. I'd often spend hours pouring over their works, and memorizing passages that seemed special to me.

I can still quote lines from Blake's childlike poems "The Lamb" and "The Tyger"; those verses showed me clearly and simply the two opposite aspects of the human spirit. And Keats' "Ode on a Grecian Urn"! How I wondered over that ending phrase: "Beauty is truth, truth beauty,' that is all ye know on earth, and all ye need to know". I hadn't ever been exposed to or considered such a proposition before, and I spent a lot of time dreaming about the implications of such a world view.

I liked the Victorian writers almost as well. Arnold, Tennyson, the Brownings! In fact, I remember getting quite infatuated with the Brownings' and their poetry to each other; many a good cry did I have over "Sonnets from the Portuguese"!

But it was the women writers that fascinated me most. George Sand and George Elliot, writing under pseudonyms in order to publish their books! Jane Austen, the Bronte sister! I marveled over the intensely romantic Emily Dickinson, whose poems were discovered in a locked box after her death; her gift of expression far beyond the limits of our experience. How I longed to be able to write with the same deep feeling and passion those women conveyed in their works!

And I tried! I attempted to write both poetry and prose, devoting much time and energy to my ambition of becoming a writer. I sent my share of verses and stories to various magazines, but never with much success, and I grew accustomed to the disappointment of receiving rejection slips in the mail.

In order to boost my morale, I often submitted my literary efforts to the school paper. It was fairly easy for me to get my work put in the paper, and this publication allowed me both the glow one gets when reading one's own name and accomplishments in print, and recognition as a well-known writer – at the convent, that is!

There was published in our school paper an article I had written about Henry Harland, a popular author of that day. As was the custom, schools exchanged their publications, and one of ours fell into the hands of a student at Holy Cross College in Massachusetts, who also liked Mr. Harland. He wrote me a letter, discussing the article and its subject. It was a long letter, an interesting and humorous one, touching on different matters.

I wasn't particularly interested in boys at this time but here was I, an ordinary high school student, receiving a letter from a young college gentleman, and that in itself was SOMETHING. Furthermore, the letter came to a girl in a school that absolutely did not allow letters from boys. Proudly, I showed my letter to a friend.

All this made me a very important person at Sinsinawa, and faster than a fire the question spreading across the school was, "Did you know that

Irene Merrill got a letter from a boy?" For don't think I kept my big news secret. It wasn't long before practically every girl in school had read, and giggled, over that letter.

But naturally, the Sisters soon got wind of this happening and I was called into the office and questioned. "Do I understand you received a letter from a boy?" My voice was most respectful. "Yes, Sister." "Has anyone else read the letter?" "Yes, Sister." "Will you please tell me who?"

Each time she repeated the same question, and I would name another girl. It seemed as if I had named a third of the girls at school who had read the letter before she abruptly stopped the questioning to request the letter. She accepted it with the promise it would be returned to me at the end of the school year. It was. That incident had a sequel many years later, but the place for that story is not here.

Unfortunately Mother's dream of having a gentle, refined lady-like daughter never came true. Though I am reluctant to admit, it was something like trying to make a silk purse from a sow's ear. Never would I have been a good advertisement for a "convent-bred" product. I came out as I went in—rough and tumble, careless and carefree—but several years older, of course. But I have always been grateful for those convent years. Except for those bouts with homesickness at the beginning of each school term, it was a very happy time of my life.

METAMORPHOSIS

Eventually a metamorphosis took place. I changed from pupil to teacher. In my day, very few girls went on to college. Only the exceptional student aspired for a higher education. After high school a young lady was more apt to set her goals on a job—or marriage. The latter preferred!

Of all jobs for women teaching was the most prestigious and did not require a college degree. Eight weeks of Summer school, however, were mandatory. If one passed the examinations at the end she was eligible to teach.

A teacher was welcome anywhere, her social standing secure—as long as she lived an exemplary life. Dancing and card-playing, forbidden by some churches, and late night hours were frowned upon. The community also took stock of the company their teacher kept. Hence many a young man, seeking a good time, might look other than in the school room for companionship. So actually there was more truth than poetry in the phrase "old maid school teacher". I knew plenty of them. I smile in remembering that a high school friend and I planned to go to Alaska when we graduated to teach. Our reason? We believed that since there were more men than women there it would be a good hunting ground for husbands. Fortunately that dream was forgotten as the years went by and we found more exciting things to take their place.

My goal was to become a Latin teacher, as Latin was my favorite subject. But an Iowa law required that any girl must teach one year in a country school before being judged ready to teach in a town or city. This policy probably was deliberately contrived as the only practical way of attracting girls to teach in the country schools where life itself was much more arduous than in the city schools.

I applied for a school about ten miles from my home town.[51] By teaching there I could board at the farm home of one of my school mates, Ina,[52] whose mother was the aunt of my "beau",[53] as we called them then, so it would be like living with friends. For room and board I paid eight dollars a month. That's right, a month! And my salary was forty dollars a month. Chicken feed, according to today's salaries. But I remember with amusement my mother's exuberance over that sum, always clothes conscious, she exclaimed, "Oh, Irene, how well you can dress on that!" Most of that money, $32 left after room and board, went for just that, clothes. By the end of my first year of teaching I was about $50 in debt, an amount which my father begrudgingly paid.

While at first it had all looked quite exciting, I found my first experience with country living to be otherwise. Although living with friends, the evenings were too long and lonesome. The mooing of the cows at milking time, the bawling of the calves being weaned from their mothers, were mournful sounds to me. Even worse was awakening each morning to the dismal groan of the cream separator coming up from the kitchen. As I crawled sleepily out of bed all I wanted was to be home.

Some scenes I remember so well from my year on that farm. For instance, flies. If you know anything about farms you know that before DDT they were wonderful breeding beds for flies. Each fall morning the screens in the back porch would be black with flies, clinging here to absorb some warmth from the house.

They would be numb with cold each morning, before the sun could thaw them out, Ina's mother would sweep them down with a broom and call the chickens. I can see those old hens yet, come running with wings outspread in their haste to gobble up those flies before they came "alive."

Then churning! The barrel churn about half the size of a regular barrel was turned by a dog on a tread mill. I never could figure out what kept that dog going round 'n round, until the butter came, without any inducement what-so-ever that I could see. It was a far easier way than my grandmother churned. There's a different splash to the cream when the butter's "come", easily recognized by the initiated. Then the dog would be stopped, the rich creamy buttermilk with its flecks of butter drawn off. The churn would be half filled with water and the dog started on his rounds again, until the butter was thoroughly washed.

The hard part came in working the butter in a big wooden bowl with a wooden paddle until every drop of water had been worked out. After that was done it was packed in crocks and stored in the cool earthen cellar until the next trip to town when it was sold. Often, if one had enough cows, the butter that was made would more than pay one's grocery bill and leave enough over for a woman to buy calico for a wrapper or some other necessity. Home-made butter, once upon a time, brought a better price than creamery butter, with some women who made a superior quality commanding a better price than others.

But I liked the occasional buggy trips to town after school with Ina to buy groceries for her mother at the country store. We'd fool around, or stroll down the board walk to the country store where we'd meet some boys and get a date for show, party, buggy ride, or in winter, sleigh ride. Generally we drove home dateless, but happy just on having broken the week's monotony.

My little one room white school house set a half mile down the road from the farm on an acre of cleared land cut out of a forest of trees that bordered a near-by river. I walked the distance each morning, regardless of weather. I had to go early enough to build a fire in the pot-bellied stove at the back of the room so it would be warm by the time the pupils arrived. Some teachers were able to pay one of their older boys to build their fires for them, but my pupils came from a neighborhood of parents who believed in letting the teacher build her own fires.

I taught all eight grades,54 with thirteen students ranging in age from those who were little more than out of diapers to those overalled boys, taller than I, and often the unruly ones. I've often wondered how I managed, but once the year started things went along fairly well. Although I never really liked teaching country school. My thoughts were generally more apt to be on Friday night when I could pack my grip and go home for the weekend.

Getting home on Fridays, and back to school on Mondays, presented such difficulties that only my homesickness could have made me go. I had two choices in getting home. I could walk the ten miles on the lonely country road, or trudge three miles back to the railroad station and wait for the ten o'clock train to come. The station would be as deserted as the desert after a sandstorm. The inevitable rusty pot-bellied stove in the center of the room kept it warm. An oil lamp in a bracket hanging from the wall provided a dim light by which I could read. I could see the lights of the town about a block away, but the steady click, click, clickety, click of the telegraph keys, broken

occasionally by the far away bark of a dog, were the only sounds. It was an isolated spot for a young woman, but in those days it was so safe that I had no thought of fear. Soon the station agent arrived, a few idlers started straggling in. At the toot of a far away whistle, I'd start to pick up my belongings to be ready when the train pulled into the station.

The ten mile walk home I attempted only in spring or fall when I felt reasonably sure of arriving home before dark. Don't get the idea I might have been able to hitch hike! Few cars were seen in that part of the country. Whatever wheeled vehicle I might see—horse 'n buggy, team and lumber wagon—would be sure to be going home, away from town, not toward it. Sometimes a friend would walk half way to meet me. Gabbing with her on the way back to town made the walk seem shorter.

Getting home was one thing, but getting back to school was quite another! I had to rise in what seemed the middle of the night each Monday morning, walk several blocks carrying my bag, and catch a train that rolled out of town around five A.M. I got off at a small country town, not yet awake, three miles from my school. From there I had to walk. I would try so hard each time to break my record but could never make more than a mile in fifteen minutes. In winter, on roads rutted with snow and ice, the wind in my face, it took much longer than that. I was always plenty glad to stop at my boarding house for breakfast and to warm up before going on to the school. Where, you will remember, I still had to build the fire to warm up the room for the pupils.

While getting to school and back did give me some problems, there were those special times when my beau would drive his little mare, Blackie, out to get me. Sometimes then, we'd go to a dance in that little country town. The hall was dusty, dreary, unadorned. The dancing, often rowdyish, was usually square dances called by a man who rattled them off so fast that only those who knew them well could understand. The music was furnished by a country fiddler, a tin-panny piano and drums. Occasionally a waltz, a two-step or the Virginia reel would be thrown in, with much foot stomping sometimes drowning out the music. But breathless, perspiring, exhausted, what a good time we had! We were never quite ready to give up and go home, even when we saw the fiddler put away his fiddle and everyone prepare to leave for the night.

Even though the best of the evening was yet to come—that long, long ride home, with the lines wrapped around the whip socket, Blackie allowed to take her own sweet time. Did my mother ever worry when it wasn't until the wee hours of the night when we reached home? Once I found her walking the floor, thinking surely there must have been an accident. She confessed later that she'd even gone so far as to wonder what dress she'd bury me in. But, more often than not, she slept through it all, unaware of my late arrival home.

One dark raining night we almost did have an accident. Rain was coming down by the buckets full when we started for home. With buggy top up, side curtains buttoned, and a heavy robe over our laps we should have been well protected. But the wind was driving the rain straight at us. No lines around the whip socket that night. With deep ditches on both sides of us, it took all our ingenuity to keep Blackie on the water-logged road, visible to us only during those sharp crackling flashes of lightening.

Finally at a horrendous crash of thunder Blackie, tired of facing into the storm, took things into her own. Before we had any idea of her intention, she swung around, down into the ditch and when fully turned, stopped dead. How she maneuvered that buggy into that ditch without upsetting us all only the gods can answer. Breathless with the unexpectedness of it, it was some time before our thoughts could focus on getting her back on the road, turned around and headed back toward home.

No trouble from there on. But I count that as the most propitious night of my life. For that was the night the gentleman proposed to me. Which is why I gave up teaching, did not become a Latin teacher, nor even the great writer I thought I would be. I became instead a farmwife, which is what I honestly had aspired to in the first place, and lived happily ever after.

But THAT is another story.

A PIN SHOWER

The home of Miss June Oppenheimer was the scene of a very pretty shower last evening given by her in honor of Miss Irene Merrill. The eight girls enjoyed the evening playing 500, after which they were invited to the dining room where a color scheme of pink was artistically wrought out in the decorations and in the dainty refreshments. Pink ribbons streamed like a shower from the chandelier to the chair of the bride-to-be, where were the gifts, all sorts of beautiful pins, each accompanied by original verse. The place cards were hearts done in pink water colors, and pink carnations were given as favors.

The eight girls who will always remember with pleasure this charming evening together are:

Josie Hanrahan   Florence Woolston
Sadie Campbell   Louise Houck
Myrtle Sullivan Irene Merrill
        June Oppenheimer
Mrs. H. G. Higbee, of Dubuque.

Merrill Family Chronology

William T. Merrill (22 July 1814-31 Dec 1878) married Rebecca Brown (1 Aug 1812-6 Jan 1883) on 20 Apr 1841 in Ludlow, VT. William has been listed as the son of Abraham Merrill (1784) and Sally Tolbert (1784) however no documents have yet been found for this and it is unknown if he was born in NH or VT. Rebecca was the daughter of Israel Putnam Brown (1781-1867) and Sally Briggs (1784-1826). Of note is that Rebecca remarried about 1881 to Ira Pinney and is buried with him. Her name appears on 1880 census for both Rochester, MN and Plymouth, VT. A news article was also found for Plymouth, VT giving an account of the house she owned being moved to a new foundation in about 1880 which may account for her being listed with her son in MN while this took place but still being listed in VT as she did own the house.

The 1845,6,7,8,9 & 50 Vermont, Town Clerk, Vital and Town Records, 1732-1857 (Windsor County, Plymouth) lists for School Dist #1: William Merrill with son Adam Merrill. In the 1850 census for Plymouth, VT, William P(T)(36) and Rebecca (30) are listed with children Adam C. (14), William Henry (8), Rebecca M. (5) & Theodore (2). It is most likely that Adam C. is actually Carlos Addison Merrill (9 Dec 1836-18 Feb 1913). No birth certificate has yet been found and it is unknown if he was the son of William by a prior marriage or an affair or possibly the son of Rebecca by an affair (see marriage date above). Carlos (or Adam) may have been born in NH as there has been reference to Sullivan, NH. The only real way to prove the lineage would be for a current Merrill male descendant of Carlos to have DNA submitted to the registry to compare with known Merrill DNA.

Carlos A. Merrill next appears in Texas, Michigan in his marriage on 29 Nov 1857 to Sarah M (A) Bishop 28 May 1835-1 Feb1913. And then in the 1860 Census for Texas, MI with his wife Sarah and his occupation listed as Farmer. Next in the 1863 consolidated census and military draft list as a farmer and married. In the 1864 tax list Carlos is still in Texas and is a horse dealer. In 1866 the tax list has Carlos in Schoolcraft, MI and a stallion dealer.
The 1870 census for Schoolcraft, MI lists Carlos, Sarah and children Addison (9), William (8), Blanch (4) and Grace (1). William being the son who would be our great grandfather. Also, in the 1870 census for LaPorte City, Indiana it lists Chas. (Carlos?) Merrill with Sarah (no children listed) and as an occupation "Hotel" with a value of $10,000 and property of $3,000. This would seem to indicate he owned the hotel. And then from sworn testimony in 1872 of Addison Merrill before the Michigan legislature he gives his residence as the Merrill House hotel in LaPorte, IN in 1871 which was owned by his father, Carlos Merrill. This seems to be the first record of Carlos entering into the hotel business but efforts to find more information about the Merrill House in LaPorte have not yet been successful.

In 1874 a Rochester, Minnesota news account said "Carlos A. Merrill from Indiana opened the Cook's Hotel as landlord" - until 1879. The 1875 Rochester Minn census lists Carlos A. Merrill (38), Sarah (40),

Addison (14), Willie (12), Blanche (9), Grace (6) and Alida (21) who is Carlos' sister from VT.

The 1880 census from Rochester, MN lists Carlos A. Merrill with his occupation as Hotel Keeper. Sarah and the children are also listed as well as Rebecca, Carlos' mother.

The 1885 Minneapolis census lists C. A. Merrill (48), his wife Sarah E. (50) and the 4 children, Addison C. (24), Wm. N. (22), Blanche (20) & Grace (16). His mother and sister are not among the list, which is lengthy (27 names) because it most likely contains all of the residents of the boarding house.

The 1879-80 Minneapolis City Directory has a C. Merrill as a boarder at the Bushnell House and a William Merrill, student, at: r.250 3rd Av.N. In the 1885-6 Minneapolis City Directory C.A.Merril is listed as proprietor of the Merrill House at: 400 6th Av.S. , A.C. Merrill is the clerk and Wm. N. Merrill is listed at: r.Merrill House. The 1886-7 Minneapolis City Directory lists Carlos A. Merrill at: r.2532 Chicago Av. with a different proprietor at the Merrill House. A.C. and Wm.N. are listed as owners of the Merrill brothers Saloon at the St.James Hotel.

The 1888-89 Directory lists Carlos A. Merrill as Proprietor of the National Hotel & the Sherman House: r.Sherman House. It is also believed that it was here that our grandmother, Irene Merrill, was born in 1888. On the1889-90 Directory Carlos A. Merrill is listed as proprietor of the National Hotel with Wm. N. Merrill as clerk of the National Hotel; 205 Washington Av.S tel 557-2. Historic records show The National Hotel was built in 1884 at 205 Washington Ave. S. and was a five floor building.

The 1890-91 Directory shows the National Hotel under new management and no listings are found for the Carlos Merrill family or the Sherman House.   It most likely was at this time that Carlos took over the Duncombe Hotel in Fort Dodge, Iowa. The 1895 census doesn't list anyone of the family in Minnesota

On 6 Sept. 1887 William N. Merrill married Sophia Mundt in Minneapolis, Hennepin, Minnesota. Witnesses were Blanche Merrill and Louisa Mundt. His brother, Addison C. Merrill married Mary E. White in 1889 in Fort Dodge, Iowa.   Unknown if any children.   He then divorced and re-married in Dec. 1894 to Lucy.   Again, unknown if any children. The Iowa 1895 census for Newell, Buena Vista County, Iowa lists Chas. (Carlos) A. Merrill (58), born Vermont, as a famer with his wife Sarah A. Merrill (59) born Michigan.   No children are listed with them. Fort Dodge is in Webster County, not Buena Vista so this is most likely the farm that Gram talks about visiting in her book. The same 1895 census for Hamilton County, Iowa lists Wm. N. Merrell (Merrill) (33), occupation as Hotel Proprietor born Michigan and Sophia (27) and Irene (6) born Minnesota.   This, of course, would be the Willson Hotel in Webster City. Also listed at the same location are 50 additional names, presumably the residents of the hotel.   Strangely among these is Carl Merrill (54) born Vermont listed as retired and wife Sarah Merrill (56).   No doubt, the names among the residents would lead to the identity of the many servants and people grandmother wrote about. Unknown why Maris Jacob Merrill (2) is NOT listed in the census.

In the Minneapolis City Directory for 1896, CA Merrill is listed as the proprietor or manager of the Windsor Hotel. This listing continued in the following years' directories until 1900. The 1901 directory says "moved to Webster City, Iowa".

The 1900 census for Webster City lists Will W. Merrill (37), Sophie (35), Irine (12) at school, J. Morris (Maris Jacob) (7), Gertrude (5), Charline (3), and Glaydis (1). Along with many servants (9) and boarders (12) Carl and Sarah Merrill are also listed with them at the Willson hotel.

AND, the 1900 census for Minneapolis at the Windsor Hotel lists Carlos (63), Sarah (65) AND Addison (39) PLUS William N. (37). No wife is shown for Addison and a margin note for Wm. reads "Iowa".

Photo- L to R, T to B:

Maris Jacob, Irene Merrill Mason, Leonard Nelson Mason, Gertrude, Herman Dietrich, Sophie, William 'Billie' Jr., William N. Sr., Charline, Barbara, Gladys, Grace, Freda.

The 1905 Iowa census lists the Merrill family at 1020 2nd Street in Webster City. Gram wrote that the large family was too much commotion for the hotel so they bought a nearby house. CA Merrill ran the Willson Hotel until 1905. William was busy developing a block of stores next to the hotel for his cigar store and other businesses.

The 1910 census lists the family still in Webster City, although not including Irene, as she was married to Leonard Mason in 1909. In February of 1913, Sarah Merrill died in her apartment over Channer Drugstore. Seventeen days later, Carlos died in the hospital from a prostate operation.

The 1914 Webster City Directory has the Wm. Merrill family still at the 1020 2nd Street address. The 1920 and 1925 census also lists the family but with fewer children each time.

The one room schoolhouse was in Eagle Grove, Iowa where Irene boarded with the Aunt of her husband to be, Annabelle (Omstead) Campbell and Arthur Campbell who had a daughter named Ina. She taught there for one year and married Leonard Mason in the Fall of 1909.

Mundt Family Chronology

Christian Mundt (1824 Frankfurt – 19 July 1868 Iowa) married Barbara Hirth (26 Dec 1832 Hockenheim – 5 May 1910 Spokane) and immigrated to the US as an elopement. Place and date of marriage have not yet been found but supposedly it took place in Dubuque, Iowa. Christian died suddenly leaving Barbara with the 6 children. Christian had been a hotel keeper, running the Diamond House in Lansing, Iowa. The children were Robertena Lena (1858-1899); Louis (1860-1894); William (1862-1930); Elizabeth 'Bertha' (1863-1894); Sophia (Gram's mother) and Louisa (1868-1931).

Barbara Hirth Mundt also had 4 brothers who immigrated to the US and 3 sisters. She managed a boarding house (possibly the Diamond House) after Christian's death for a short time. I believe she relied on the brothers' help later on and may have even lived with them for a time before moving to Spokane, Washington to live with her daughter Louisa.

Robertena married Earl (Charles) Dietrich in Minneapolis and had two children; Charles and Herman. Herman lived with the Merrills after Robertena's untimely death. Louis had no children. William married Catherine (from Germany) and had three children, George, Louis and Irene in Washington. Elizabeth 'Bertha' married John Kelty in Minneapolis and had three children, Louis, John and Florence, the latter also lived with the Merrills after their mother's untimely death. Young John and Louis moved to S.Dakota and were living with another unrelated family. Louisa married Herman Lang and had four children in Washington: Lawrence, Verona, Randolph and Adolph. And of course Sophia, Irene's mother, who married William Merrill.

I have had considerable success at finding the original documents to prove many of the above facts and have saved them all along with photographs and some are in the family tree, on line at Ancestry.com and the LDS website. I also have sourced some of the information and photographs to include in the book from the Iowa GenWeb Project, the Kendall Young Librarian in Webster City and the Hennepin County Library in Minnesota.

APPENDIX
Willson Hotel from the 1895 Iowa Census

Name	Sex	Age		Name	Sex	Age
Wm N Merrell	M	33		Alpha Ford	F	23
Sophia Merrell	F	27		Geo Kernan	M	27
Irene Merrell	F	6		Mary Halken	F	17
Burt F Keltz	M	21		Gertrude Mcfarland	F	16
Amanda Johnson	F	35		M C Mccoy	M	35
Jacob M Funk #30	M	60		Alice Echelberger	F	18
Geo H Renicker #17	M	43		Mary Graft	F	18
Chas H Slack	M	23		Jas Patel	M	18
Geo K Nairn	M	38		Julie Lynch	F	24
W J Selby	M	26		Archie Kearns #21	M	19
Wm B Kearns #20	M	28		Mary Cooper	F	17
Anna K Kearns #19	F	28		Marie Mc Coy	F	17
Mattie Holt	F	30		Frankie Welsh	F	28
E C Baily	M	35		Agness Rooney	F	23
E Skewis	F	32		Bertha Lande	F	18
Edward S Wheeler	M	38		Anna Lande	F	20
Elizabeth Wheeler	F	48		Nettie Solso	F	20
Geo H Grant	M	35		Hannah Oleson	F	19
M Hilbert	M	45		Ed E Buzick	M	20
E P Fuller	M	40		Matilda Bankston #15	F	20
Wilson R Warfield	M	45		Nels Nelson	M	21
J B De Val Court	M	27		Cora Cook	F	18
U L Cherrier	M	35		Saml Mc Clure	M	31
Carl Merril *	M	54		Lillie L Mc Clure	F	29
Sarah Merril *	F	56		Olive Mc Clure	F	19
John W Kelley	M	28		J W Jenney	M	28
Joe Wheeler	M	22				

Willson Hotel from the 1900 US Census

Relation	Name	Sex	Age	Relation	Name	Sex	Age
Head	Will W Merrill	M	37	Boarder	Edward E Fox	M	32
Wife	Sophie Merrill	F	35	Boarder	Fred Girniorn	M	24
Daugh.	Irine Merrill	F	12	Cook	Dollie Cerrais	F	27
Son	J Morris Merrill	M	7	Cook	Laura Fassett	F	26
Daugh.	Gertrude Merrill	F	5	ChmbMaid	Matilda Bankston #15	F	27
Daugh.	Charline Merrill	F	3	Cook	Nellie Peterson	F	26
Daugh.	Claydis Merrill	F	1	Waitress	Mary Peterson	F	20
Niece	Florence Kelty	F	14	Waitress	Bertha Landu	F	24
Servant	William A Foster	M	26	Waitress	Christa Johnston	F	25
Servant	Elwood J Kidder	M	23	Servant	Mattie Knudson	F	27
Servant	Charles Blazris	M	20	Servant	Lena Munson	F	25
Servant	George Barber	M	38	Servant	I* Middleton	F	25
Boarder	Jacob M Funk	M	71	Servant	Bertha Jacobson	F	25
Boarder	J B Devalcourt	M	32	Servant	Jennie Stone	F	26
Boarder	John P Metcalf	M	62				

Willson Hotel from the 1905 Iowa Census

Johnson, W.H.

Carlson, Al   M

Foster, Frank   M

Thompson, Tellie   F

Hamcock, W.B.   M

McCostra, Kate   F

Schrader, Mary   F

Jones, Ernest   M

Haines, May   F

Reineker, Geo. H. #17   M

Toskey, R.

Bingston, Tillie #15   F

Holman, Glen   M

Myers, Tillie   F

Merrel, C.A. *   M

Merrell, Sarah A. *   F

Smith, Bertha   F

Seltz, Robt.   M

Baldwin, Eugene   M

Wallace, Henry   M

THE WILLSON

W. N. MERRILL, PROP.

Christmas Dinner, A. D. 1912

Oyster Cocktail

Mulligatawney   Consomme Royal

Celery   Olives   Radishes   Sliced Cucumbers

Mexican Chili Con Carne

Boiled Sugar Cured Ham—Champagne Sauce

Candied Sweet Potatoes

Emince of Chicken—a la Prett

Prime Ribs of Beef—au jus   Roast Young Turkey—Oyster Dressing

Mashed Potatoes   Cranberry Sauce

Peach Compote with Fruited Rice

Patties of Calf Brains   French Peas

Braised Domestic Duck—Apple Sauce

Spinach   Mock Chestnut Dressing

Lobster en Mayonnaise

Apple Pie   Pumpkin Pie   Mince Pie

American Cheese   Salted Wafers

English Plum Pudding—Hard Sauce

Chocolate Ice Cream   Assorted Cake

Mixed Nuts   Fruit   Sweet Cider

Coffee   Tea   Cocoa   Milk

50 ¢

MAP OF IOWA MINN WISC
1893

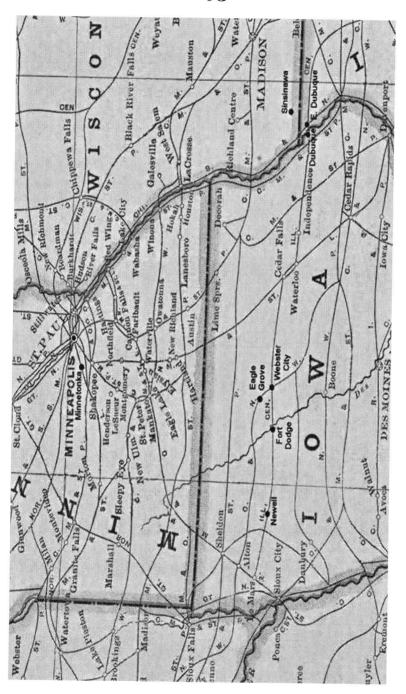

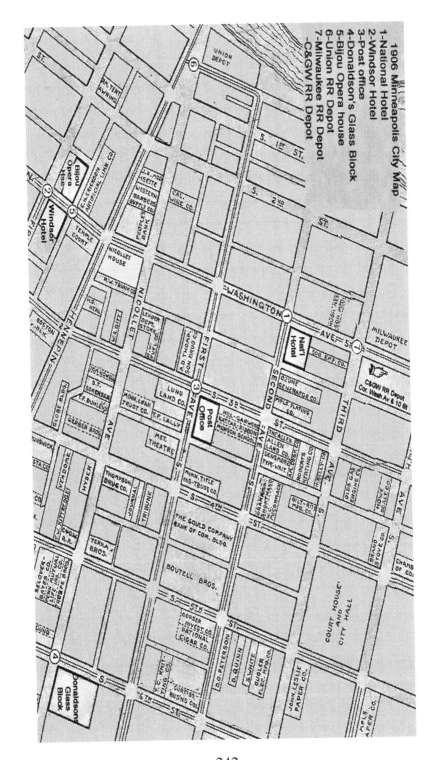

1906 Minneapolis City Map
1-National Hotel
2-Windsor Hotel
3-Post office
4-Donaldson's Glass Block
5-Bijou Opera house
6-Union RR Depot
7-Milwaukee RR Depot
-C&GW RR Depot

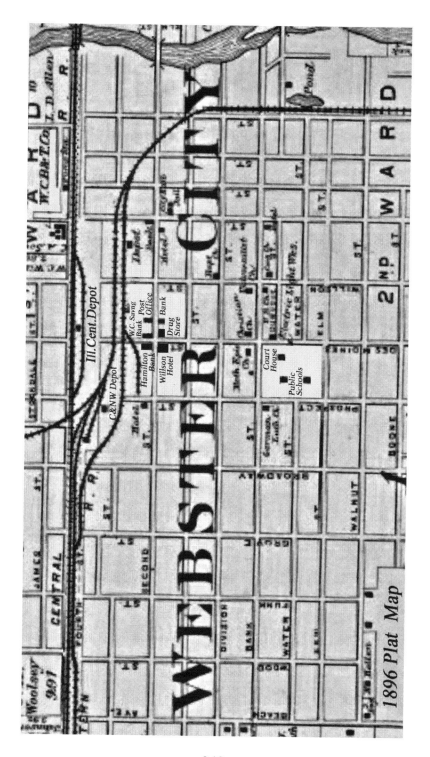

1896 Plat Map

243

IMAGES

NOTES

[1] Carlos Addison (Adam) Merrill; 9 Dec 1836-18 Feb 1913

[2] Sarah M (A) Bishop; 28 May 1835-1 Feb 1913

[3] Calvin Coolidge, son of Calvin Sr. on 3 Mar.1844 married Sally A. Brown, sister to Rebecca Brown Merrill, Carlos' mother.

[4] Carlos' father died in 1878, long after Carlos had moved to Michigan and his mother only remarried in 1881

[5] Documents show he ran or owned the Merrill House in LaPorte City, Indiana in 1871

[6] In 1874 a Rochester, Minnesota news account had "Carlos A. Merrill from Indiana opened the Cook's Hotel as landlord"

[7] born in the National Hotel located at 205 Washington Av.S. (1884-1929)

[8] Duncombe Hotel in Fort Dodge, Iowa about 1890

[9] Iowa 1895 census for Newell, Buena Vista County, Iowa lists Chas. (Carlos) A. Merrill (58), born Vermont, as a famer with his wife Sarah A. Merrill (59) born Michigan, presumed to be his farm

[10] farrowed - When a sow gives birth to a new litter of piglets.

[11] Duncombe Hotel in Fort Dodge, Iowa about 1890

[12] June M. Oppenheimer born 23 Nov 1887 daughter of Joseph & Freda Weiler Oppenheimer married Mose J. Frisch on 19 Sept 1911 in Webster City.

[13] Census lists for 1895, 1900 & 1905 list a number of the people mentioned , see pages 239,240

[14] Dick .... head cook

[15] Matilda "Tillie" Bankston   chambermaid

[16] martinet - a strict disciplinarian.

[17] George Renicker   yardman, driver

[18] Bridget 'Bedelia' M. Cayton   black dishwasher   married Herman Mitchell in 1898 had a son Stephen; moved to S.Dakota – in 1910 census w/ husband

[19] Anna K. (Stafford) Kearns   head waitress

[20] William B. Kearns   day clerk 911 1st St. 1905 census

[21] Archie Kearns   porter & man of all trades

[22] Joe Wheeler   depot driver   murdered Sept.1910 in Mankato,Minn.

[23] Whist - English trick taking card game, the precursor to Bridge.

[24] Cousin Ella .... possibly a sister to grandmother Merrill (Bishop)

[25] propitiously - presenting favorable circumstances.

[26] leghorn hat - a flat crown hat made from dried and bleached wheat straw

[27] Minnie Willson, wife of Frank Willson

[28] This is more "family lore" than proof and is doubtful as there were many previous settlers in Webster City

[29] Jacob Funk is listed in the numerous Census as a resident of the Willson Hotel and owned numerous parcels of land in Webster City

[30] his actual birth name was Maris Jacob Merrill

[31] Robertena Mundt Dietrich

[32] interlocutor - performer in a minstrel show who is placed midway between the end men and engages in banter with them

[33] bête noire - a person or thing that one particularly dislikes.

[34] emetic – a substance that causes vomiting

[35] expectorated – spit from the mouth

[36] Louisa (Mundt) Lang m. Herman Lang 1889 Spokane, Washington

[37] The Windsor Hotel was on the corner of Washington & 1st Av.N.

[38] Donaldson's Glass Block Dept.Store – built 1887, demolished 1981

[39] Grace Merrill m. Fred E. Wheaton in Fort Dodge, Iowa in 1890

[40] Robertena Mundt married Earl Charles Dietrich and she died in 1899

[41] Earl Charles J. Dietrich lived at 2210 S. 9th St., Minneapolis

[42] The Minnetonka House name was soon changed to the Lake Hotel and after 1903 to Tonka Bay Hotel.

[43] the Boone River, primary waterway in Webster City

[44] The Buffalo Bill Wild West show came to Webster City in 1899

[45] In later life, Grandmother collected elephant statues and filled her shelves with them and they became her prized possessions.

[46] Florence Kelty daughter of Elizabeth 'Bertha' & John Kelty

[47] Mary E. (May) White married Addison Merrill Dec. 1894

[48] St. Clara Academy founded by Father Samuel Mazzuchelli and after his death the Dominican Sisters moved it to Sinsinawa, Wis.

[49] St. Clara is located in Sinsinawa, Wisconsin. East Dubuque is in Illinois, across the Mississippi from Dubuque, Iowa and south of Sinsinawa..

[50] Menominee, Illinois is a small town south of the Wisconsin line.

[51] Eagle Grove, Wright, Iowa one room school near the Boone River

[52] Ina A. Campbell born May 1886 daughter of Annabelle (Annie) Omstead & Arthur L. Campbell

[53] Leonard Nelson Mason born 28 October 1887 Webster City, Iowa son of Clarissa Omstead & Bridgeman Camden Mason

[54] Irene taught school from September 1908 to May 1909, 1 year.

26421282R00145

Made in the USA
Charleston, SC
07 February 2014